REFERENCE GUIDES IN LITERATURE
Joseph Katz, General Editor
JOHN OSBORNE, NO. 2

JOHN OSBORNE:

A REFERENCE GUIDE

Cameron Northouse

Thomas P. Walsh

G. K. HALL & CO., 70 LINCOLN STREET, BOSTON, MASS. 1974

Library of Congress Cataloging in Publication Data

Northouse, Cameron.
   John Osborne: a reference guide.

   (Reference guides in American literature, no. 2)
    1. Osborne, John, 1929-   --Bibliography.
I. Walsh, Thomas P., joint author.
Z8647.54.N67   016.822'9'14   74-14966
ISBN 0-8161-1152-9

Introduction

Since May 8, 1956, when <u>Look Back in Anger</u> was
first produced at the Royal Court Theatre, John Osborne
has been at the center of controversy. Questions that
arose at that time--Is John Osborne the embodiment of
the "new" British dramatist? Is his work sham or
prophecy? Social criticism or misanthropy? A scream
of anguish and despair or the outrage of a trivial and
inconsequential mind?--have never met with any clear
resolution. In fact, they may persist more widely
today. Osborne has not only permitted this controversy
to revolve around him, but has frequently inflamed it
by lashing out at his critics and countrymen, both in
his plays and elsewhere, with an overpowering poignancy
and sense of conviction combined with an artful use of
the barbed phrase. Apparently, he is willing to open
himself to attack at every turn and has received a most
willing audience.

Osborne has been remarkably productive. Twenty-two
of his plays have been produced, including two television dramas. He has written five screenplays, con-
tributed numerous articles and commentaries on the
theatre and contemporary society, participated in numerous social and political protests, acted in at least one
movie ("Carter") and several plays, led battles against
the newspaper drama critics, and has been involved in a
succession of marriages and divorce cases.

The purpose of this bibliography is to present a
convenient list of Osborne's works and to trace, by

INTRODUCTION

chronology and annotation, the history of the public
response to his work. Thus, the first section is de-
voted to Osborne's works. It lists in chronological
order his dramatic works, screenplays, and miscella-
neous prose. The second section gives a year-by-year
listing of critical and biographical works about
Osborne. Under each year, the criticism is subdivided
into "BOOKS" (A) and "ARTICLES" (B) and enumerated in
these subdivisions alphabetically. Unauthored articles
have been alphabetized by journal title and listed by
date of publication within the specific journal title.
This manner of presentation allows the reader of the
bibliography to discover the amount of commentary on
Osborne in any particular year, its temper, and its
mode (books, articles, or reviews). Also, this method
demonstrates any fluctuations in the amount of criticism from one year to another, over a selected period,
and throughout Osborne's career. Access to authors and
critical articles in books dealing with Osborne's individual works is provided in the Index.

Following the second section of the bibliography
is a selected list of non-English criticism on Osborne.
In this list, all of the known critical books and articles that comment at some length on Osborne have been
included, but reviews of the continental productions of
his plays have not been cited.

The intention behind the annotations in section two
is to provide a brief abstract of the content of a particular article or book. In other words, there has been
no conscious attempt to judge the value of a comment on
Osborne. The purpose is to locate references and indi-
cate their content, not guide those who use the bibliography to think of Osborne or his critics in a special
fashion. In cases where the original critical document
has been inaccessible and a reprinted source has been
used, the bibliographic reference is followed by an as-
terisk (*).

Introduction

The body of the bibliography is followed by the "Index."

In all bibliographies, especially those on contemporary authors, it is necessary to offer an apology. This bibliography is intended to cover John Osborne's career from 1956 to 1972, but no doubt items have been missed. Moreover, Osborne and his critics have certainly not ceased to publish as of 1972. Therefore, it is important to recognize that no claim is extended other than that this bibliography might serve a utilitarian purpose. Any comments on items that have been neglected would be most welcomed.

Contents

JOHN OSBORNE: A REFERENCE GUIDE

BY JOHN OSBORNE

A. Plays

1 "The Devil Inside." (Produced in 1949)

2 "Personal Enemy." (Coauthored with Anthony Creighton and produced in 1953)

3 Look Back in Anger. London: Faber and Faber, 1957. New York: Criterion Books, 1957. New York: S. G. Phillips, 1957. Chicago: Dramatic, 1957

4 The Entertainer. London: Faber and Faber, 1957. New York: Criterion Books, 1958

5 Epitaph for George Dillon. London: Faber and Faber, 1958. New York: Criterion Books, 1958. (Coauthored with Anthony Creighton)

6 Three Plays. New York: Criterion Books, 1959

7 The World of Paul Slickey. London: Faber and Faber, 1958. New York: Criterion Books, 1961

8 A Subject of Scandal and Concern: A Play for Television. London: Faber and Faber, 1961

9 Luther. London: Faber and Faber, 1961. New York: Criterion Books, 1962. Chicago: Dramatic, 1961

1

John Osborne: A Reference Guide

BY JOHN OSBORNE

10 Plays for England: Under Plain Cover and The Blood
    of the Bamburgs. London: Faber and Faber,
    1963. New York: Criterion Books, 1964

11 Inadmissable Evidence. London: Evans Brothers,
    1965. London: Faber and Faber, 1965. New York:
    Grove Press, 1965

12 A Bond Honoured. London: Faber and Faber, 1966

13 A Patriot for Me. London: Faber and Faber, 1966.
    New York: Random House, 1970

14 Plays for England (Under Plain Cover and The Blood
    of the Bamburgs) and The World of Paul Slickey.
    New York: Grove Press, 1966

15 Time Present and The Hotel in Amsterdam. London:
    Faber and Faber, 1968

16 The Right Prospectus: A Play for Television. Lon-
    don: Faber and Faber, 1970

17 Very Like a Whale. London: Faber and Faber, 1971

18 West of Suez. London: Faber and Faber, 1971

19 Four Plays: West of Suez, A Patriot for Me, Time
    Present, The Hotel in Amsterdam. New York:
    Dodd, 1972

20 Hedda Gabler. London: Faber and Faber, 1972

21 The Gift of Friendship: A Play for Television.
    London: Faber and Faber, 1972

22 "A Sense of Detachment." (Produced in 1972)

JOHN OSBORNE: A REFERENCE GUIDE

BY JOHN OSBORNE

B. Screenplays

1 "Look Back in Anger." A Woodfall production in
    1959; directed by Tony Richardson; screenplay by
    Nigel Kneale with additional dialogue by John
    Osborne

2 "The Entertainer." A Woodfall production in 1960;
    directed by Tony Richardson; screenplay by John
    Osborne and Nigel Kneale

3 "Tom Jones." A Woodfall production in 1962;
    directed by Tony Richardson; screenplay by John
    Osborne. Published version: New York: Grove
    Press, 1964

4 "The Charge of the Light Brigade." A Woodfall pro-
    duction in 1968; directed by Tony Richardson;
    screenplay by John Osborne and Charles Wood

5 "Inadmissable Evidence." A Woodfall production in
    1968; directed by Anthony Page; screenplay by
    John Osborne

C. Miscellaneous Prose

1 "Letter to the Editor." Spectator, CXCVIII (April
    12, 1957), 486

2 "The Writer and His Age." London Magazine, IV (May,
    1957), 47-49

3 "Introduction" in International Theatre Annual,
    Number Two. Ed. Harold Hobson. London: Calder,
    1957

4 "They Call It Cricket" in Declaration. Ed. Tom
    Maschler. New York: McGibbon and Kee, 1958

John Osborne: A Reference Guide

BY JOHN OSBORNE

5   "Sex and Failure" in The Beat Generation. Eds.
      Gene Feldman and Max Greenberg. New York:
      Citadel, 1958

6   "The Epistle to the Philistines." London Tribune
      (May 13, 1960), p.9

7   "Threat to a Theatre for Nottingham." London Times
      (June 4, 1960), p.7d
          Letter to the editor also signed by others.

8   "That Awful Museum." Twentieth Century, CLXIX
      (February, 1961), 212-216

9   "Revolt in Cuba." London Times (April 19, 1961),
      p.13e
          Letter to the editor signed by others.

10 "A Letter to My Fellow Countrymen." London Tribune
      (August 18, 1961), p.11

11 "Dr. Agostinho Neto." London Times (October 2,
      1961), p.13d
          Letter to the editor signed by others.

12 "Berliner Ensemble." London Times (September 5,
      1963), p.13d

13 "On Critics and Criticism." London Telegraph
      (August 28, 1966), p.6

14 "Trial of Two Rolling Stones: Informing the Police."
      London Times (July 4, 1957), p.11c

15 "Intellectuals and Just Causes: A Symposium."
      Encounter, XXIX (September, 1967), 3-4

4

BY JOHN OSBORNE

16 "On the Thesis Business and the Seekers After Bare
    Approximate: On the Rights of the Audience and
    the Wink and the Promise of the Well-Made Play."
    London Times (October 14, 1967), p.20c

17 Writers' Theatre. Eds. Keith Waterhouse and Willis
    Hall. London: Heinemann, 1967
       A prefatory comment to the second act of The
    Entertainer.

18 "Playwrights and South Africa." London Times (May
    16, 1968), p.13e

19 "A Working Man." London Times (September 2, 1968),
    p.7d

20 "Transatlantic Air Race." London Times (May 12,
    1969), p.11

John Osborne: A Reference Guide

A. Books--1956

None

B. Articles--1956

1 BARBER, JOHN. "The Bitter Young Man--Like Thou-
        sands." London Daily Express (May 9, 1956),
        p.3
            Look Back in Anger is an expression of the
    common frustration of today's youth.

2 BEAVEN, JOHN. "Unlucky Jim." Twentieth Century,
        CLX (July, 1956), 72-74
            The initial critical rejections of Osborne's
    Look Back in Anger were due to the emotional
    exhaustion of effect, and the later praising re-
    views were mainly due to Osborne's age, an
    attempt to make him into the new young hope for
    English theatre. Compares Osborne to Williams
    and contrasts him with Amis.

3 GIBBS, PATRICK. "Study of an Exhibitionist." Lon-
        don Daily Telegraph and Morning Post (May 9,
        1956), p.8
            What Jimmy Porter's "predicament was apart
    from the hint that he was 'born out of his
    time,' I found difficult to decide. He was,
    perhaps, a character who should have gone to a

7

B3   ABOUT JOHN OSBORNE (1956)

GIBBS, PATRICK (cont.)
    psychiatrist rather than have come to a drama-
    tist—not at any rate to one writing his first
    play."

4 GRANGER, D. "Themes for New Voices." London Maga-
       zine, III (December, 1956), 41-47
       Discussion of the new playwrights and their
    sudden, remarkable appeal. Look Back in Anger
    has had a great effect on contemporary society,
    especially the young, but the social situation
    has also greatly influenced the play.

5 HEWES, HENRY. "Castles May Crumble." Saturday Re-
       view, IXL (October 13, 1956), 30
       Short review praising Osborne for his real-
    istic presentation of distress in Look Back in
    Anger.

6 HOPE-WALLACE, PHILLIP. "First Play by Young
       Author." Manchester Guardian (May 9, 1956),
       p.5
       Look Back in Anger is a "strongly felt but
    muddled first drama," but is evidence that
    Osborne will become a full-fledged playwright.
    Compares the play to Strindberg's work and A
    Streetcar Named Desire.

7 KEOWN, ERIC. "At the Play." Punch, CCXXX (May 16,
       1956), 606
       The play shows an influence from Freud and
    "an over-dose of Tennessee Williams." Jimmy
    Porter wallows in self-pity and is a thoroughly
    unsympathetic character. Although Look Back in
    Anger is a failure, Osborne has the potential
    for a powerful theatrical achievement.

8   "Table Talk." London Observer (June 3, 1956), p.8
        Biographical article stressing Osborne's
    level headed reaction to Look Back in Anger's
    success.

9   "The Arts." London Times (May 9, 1956), p.3d
        There is a good deal of violent writing in
    Osborne's Look Back in Anger. The author must
    be considered as a spokesman for the postwar
    generation, at least he considers himself to be.
    "Its total gesture is altogether inadequate."

10 LUSELLI, JOHN. "A Would Be Quixote in a Land With-
    out Windmills." Reporter, XV (October 18,
    1956), 33-35
        Long review of Osborne's Look Back in Anger
    discussing the popularity of production, its
    faults and successes, and why it is a reflec-
    tion of the contemporary English social deca-
    dence. The life of Jimmy Porter is one of in-
    effectual action, frustration, and denial of
    hope.

11 SIMMS, MADELEINE B. "In Re: Jimmy Porter."
    Reporter, XV (November 15, 1956), 7
        A response to John Luselli's review of Look
    Back in Anger. Simms finds Jimmy Porter to be
    atypical in English society, Look Back in Anger
    to be "intellectually facile and morally
    sterile," and both are only indicative of the
    degenerate nature of the English theatre and
    the critical standards of those who have
    praised it.

12   SPENDER, STEPHEN. "Notes from a Diary." Encounter,
         VII (August, 1956), 71.
             Look Back in Anger is the "nearest thing to
         true poetic drama" than anything on the English
         stage for years. The play may seem confused,
         but that is in the nature of an angry response.

13   TYNAN, KENNETH. "The Voice of the Young." London
         Observer (May 3, 1956), p.8. Reprinted in
         Tynan on Theatre and Curtains.
             High praise for Look Back in Anger and Os-
         borne's ability as a dramatist. He has become
         the spokesman for the disenchanted in Great
         Britain. The play is "best young play of its
         decade."

14   WORSLEY, T. C. "A Test Case." New Statesman, LI
         (May 19, 1956), 566.
             Osborne depicts a reality seldom seen on the
         stage and a convincing contemporary idiom. But
         Look Back in Anger suffers from dramatic errors,
         especially the false reconciliation at the end.

15   YOUNG, WAYLAND. "London Letter." Kenyon Review,
         XVII (Autumn, 1956), 642-647.
             Look Back in Anger is a revolutionary step
         for the British theatre. It is a play that
         says things that were taboo in 1946. Includes
         some comments on Osborne's suspected Freudian-
         isms.

A. Books--1957

None

B. Articles--1957

1 ASTON, FRANK. "Fine Acting Fails to Stir Dull
       Play." New York World-Telegram (October 2,
       1957)·* Reprinted in New York Theatre Critics'
       Reviews, XVIII, (October 7, 1957), 244
          Look Back in Anger is baffling, but the act-
       ing is good.

2 ATKINSON, BROOKS. "Theatre: A Vivid Play." New
       York Times (October 2, 1957), p.28:2. Re-
       printed in New York Theatre Critics' Reviews,
       XVIII, (October 7, 1957), 245
          The play and Osborne himself lack a "reason-
       able approach to life," but Look Back in Anger
       is well written and forceful, and a play which
       will drive the complacent from the theatre.

3 _____. "Look Back in Anger." New York Times (Octo-
       ber 13, 1957), II, p.1:1
          Praises Osborne for superb writing in Look
       Back in Anger and the creation of Jimmy Porter
       as a stylistic symbol of alienation. Osborne,
       however, needs more talent as a craftsman. The
       play is compared to Williams and Odets.

4 BARBER, JOHN. "A Born Dramatist Offers the Proof."
       London Daily Express (February 27, 1957), p.7
          Epitaph for George Dillon proves that Osborne
       is a "dramatist born."

5 _____. "Yes, This Is Olivier in Osborne's New
       Play." London Daily Express (April 11, 1957),
       p.3

_____. (cont.)
Osborne's study of Archie Rice's life is
"superbly observed; it fascinates."

6 CHAPMAN, JOHN. "Osborne's <u>Look Back in Anger</u> Puts
    Drama Season on Its Toes." <u>New York Daily News</u>
    (October 2, 1957).* Reprinted in <u>New York</u>
    <u>Theatre Critics' Reviews</u>, XVIII (October 7,
    1957), 246
        Jimmy Porter is an angry young man, but the
    play is not angry. Instead, it is "funny,"
    dramatically profound, and meaningful. "Os-
    borne is a showman as well as a cynic."

7 CLURMAN, HAROLD. "Theatre." <u>Nation</u>, CLXXXV (Octo-
    ber 19, 1957), 272. Reprinted in Clurman's
    <u>Lies Like Truth</u> and <u>John Osborne: LOOK BACK IN</u>
    <u>ANGER, A Casebook</u>.
        Discusses the effect of <u>Look Back in Anger</u>
    on the British theatre, its anticipated effect
    on Broadway, the character of Jimmy Porter, and
    the social content of the play's comment on
    class strife. The play is not realism, but "a
    theatrical stylization of ideas about reality
    in which perceptive journalism is made to flash
    on the stage by a talent for histrionic gesture
    and vivid elocution.

8 COLEMAN, ROBERT. "<u>Back in Anger</u> Is a Portrait of a
    Heel." <u>New York Daily Mirror</u> (October 2,
    1957).* Reprinted in <u>New York Theatre Critics'</u>
    <u>Reviews</u>, XVIII (October 7, 1957), 243
        Osborne and <u>Look Back in Anger</u> have merit,
    but the play is severely flawed and will not
    succeed in America to the extent it did in
    Europe.

9   COOKE, ALISTAIR. "An Angry Young Man on Broadway."
    Manchester Guardian (October 3, 1957), p.9
         A summary of the New York critics' reactions
    to Osborne's Look Back in Anger.

10 DARLINGTON, W. A. "Unlucky But Too Sorry." London
    Daily Telegraph and Morning Post (February 2,
    1957), p.10
         George Dillon is pitted against a world
    totally alien to himself. The authors' charac-
    ters are "truly and deeply depressing."

11 _____. "A Fine Study by Laurence Olivier." London
    Daily Telegraph and Morning Post (April 11,
    1957), p.10
         Osborne's play is evidence of his dramatic
    talent and clearly shows that he writes with
    background as an actor in mind.

12 DEMPSEY, D. "Most Angry Fella." New York Times
    Magazine (October 20, 1957), VI, pp. 22, 25-27
         Portrait of Osborne denying the "angry young
    man" designation, discussing Look Back in Anger,
    and his denial to commit himself to any politi-
    cal or social dogma.

13 DOBREE, BONAMY. "No Man's Land." Sewanee Review,
    LXV (1957), 309-316
         General review article on a number of publi-
    cations by members of the angry young man move-
    ment; praise for Osborne and Look Back in Anger.

14 DRIVER, TOM F. "Poor Squirrels." Christian Cen-
    tury, LXXIV (October 23, 1957), 1262-1263
         Look Back in Anger is "the story of a delib-
    erate regression into a screeching, primitive
    yet passionless existence." From this environ-
    ment there is no possibility for a meaningful
    redemption.

15 FINDLATER, RICHARD. "The Angry Young Man." <u>New York Times</u> (September 29, 1957), II, p.1:6
    Biographical articles on Osborne discussing his rather vague political stance, the theatre, his dramatic background, and his family history.

16 GIBBS, WOLCOTT. "Two Very Sad Young Men." <u>New Yorker</u>, XXXIII (October 12, 1957), 93-94
    Praises the dialogue, but criticizes the intrusion of self-pity into the play's action. <u>Look Back in Anger</u> produces a diatribe against almost everything.

17 HANCOCK, ROBERT. "Anger." <u>Spectator</u>, CXCVIII (April 5, 1957), 438-439
    Biographical information on Osborne, which relies primarily on factual material coupled with the playwright's vague comments on his work and the public reaction it has received. (See Osborne's reply in the <u>Spectator</u>, April 12, 1957, B).

18 HARTLEY, ANTHONY. "Angry Romantic." <u>Spectator</u>, CXCVIII (May 18, 1957), 688
    <u>Look Back in Anger</u> is a rare play because it is one of the few good first plays by a young British dramatist, and it is a convincing portrayal of contemporary life.

19 HAYES, RICHARD. "The Last Romantic." <u>Commonweal</u>, LXVII (November 22, 1957), 208-209
    <u>Look Back in Anger</u> is a conglomeration of obsession and selfishness, private fantasies, and fervent clamor. "Mr. Osborne's idea of the human is flippant and tedious."

20 ____. "The Last Romantic II." Commonweal, LXVII
    (November 29, 1957), 232-233
        A continuation of Hayes' attack on Look Back
    in Anger.

21 HEWES, HENRY. "Fifteen Turns in the Theatre Royal."
    Saturday Review, XL (May 11, 1957), 26
        The play is Osborne's criticism of Britain's
    reverence for tradition. The Entertainer pro-
    vides Olivier with his "only great modern per-
    formance."

22 ____. "The Unquiet Englishman." Saturday Review,
    XL (October 12, 1957), 30
        Praises Osborne as the first notable play-
    wright to emerge since Williams and Miller.
    Look Back in Anger is uncompromising and accu-
    rate in its social criticism and important for
    its expression of disillusionment.

23 HOLLIS, CHRISTOPHER. "Keeping Up With the Rices."
    Spectator, CXCIX (October 18, 1957), 504-505
        The Entertainer and Look Back in Anger are
    not about a revolt of the lower against the
    higher class, "but a revolt of those who have
    come . . . within sight of a literary and cul-
    tured life, but who have found themselves
    barred from a proper share in that life."

24 HOLLOWAY, JOHN. "Tank in the Stalls: Notes on the
    School of Anger." Hudson Review, X (Autumn,
    1957), 424-429
        A general discussion of the angry young men
    and the suspected rise of a new type of hero.
    This "new" phenomenon really began with H. G.
    Wells in Kipps and Mr. Polly.

25 KERR, WALTER. "Look Back in Anger." New York
      Herald-Tribune (October 2, 1957), p.16. Re-
      printed in New York Theatre Critics' Reviews,
      XVIII (October 7, 1956), 245
        By dealing with contemporary social matters
      in a novel way, Osborne has opened a new series
      of possibilities for the theatre. He has shown
      himself to be a writer of great ability.

26 _____. "Theater: Anger from England in a Drama by
      John Osborne." New York Herald-Tribune (October
      13, 1957), IV, p.1. Reprinted in Kerr's The
      Theater in Spite of Itself.
        Praises Osborne for providing in Look Back in
      Anger a comment on the meaning behind the
      anguish of the beat generation: a need and de-
      sire for direction in life, but the failure to
      find it.

27 "A Snarling Success." Life, XLIII (October 14,
      1957), 141-142
        The emotional effect of Osborne's Look Back
      in Anger is great.

28 "Writer Not Angry Now." Life, XLIII (October 14,
      1957), 146
        Brief biographical article discussing Os-
      borne's first day in the United States,
      Laurence Olivier, and other current topics.

29 "Undergraduate Premiere." London Times (February
      27, 1957), p.3c
        Epitaph for George Dillon is not a good play,
      but an "exercise" in which Osborne developed
      the character of Jimmy Porter.

30 "Playwright Seeks Divorce." <u>London Times</u> (February
        28, 1957), p.4c
            Osborne seeks divorce from his wife Pamela.

31 "Sir Laurence Olivier's Next Part." <u>London Times</u>
        (March 8, 1957), p.3f
            Olivier accepts a role in Osborne's <u>The En-
        tertainer</u>.

32 "<u>Look Back in Anger</u>: Revival at the Royal Court
        Theatre." <u>London Times</u> (March 12, 1957), p.3e
            <u>Look Back in Anger</u> is revived with a new
        cast. The popularity of the play is compared
        to Coward's <u>The Vortex</u>.

33 "First Night in London." <u>London Times</u> (March 13,
        1957), p.3b
            Lists the cast of <u>The Entertainer</u>.

34 "Decree Nisi For Playwright." <u>London Times</u> (April
        10, 1957), p.6f
            Osborne granted divorce because of Pamela's
        adultery.

35 "<u>Look Back in Anger</u> in Sweden." <u>London Times</u> (May
        13, 1957), p.14b
            Short report describing the great popularity
        of Osborne's play in Sweden.

36 "<u>Look Back in Anger</u> to be Done in Moscow." <u>London
        Times</u> (May 31, 1957), p.5a
            Osborne's play to be performed at the World
        Youth Festival in Moscow in July, 1957.

37 "Brief Honeymoon for Author and Bride." <u>London
        Times</u> (August 14, 1957), p.4g
            Osborne married to Mary Ure.

38 "Palace Theatre." London Times (September 11, 1957),
     p.3e
          This revived production of Look Back in Anger
     shows a high degree of quality acting and an
     element of compassion in Osborne.

39 "Look Back in Anger in New York." London Times
     (October 3, 1957), p.7d
          Notes the drama critics' praise of Osborne's
     play in its opening New York performance.

40 "Sweete Alisoun." London Times Literary Supplement
     (January 25, 1957), p.49
          Much discussion has been given to the de-
     cline of the hero in modern writing, but the
     heroine has also suffered. Alison Porter in
     Look Back in Anger is indicative of the
     heroine's decline.

41 LEWIS, THEOPHILUS. "Theatre." America, XCVII
     (November 2, 1957), 146-147
          Generally favorable of Look Back in Anger.
     Jimmy Porter is an impressive character because
     we share "his dissatisfaction with an age that
     seems to be drifting toward nihilism."

42 LUCAS, BARBARA. "Looking Back at The Entertainer."
     Twentieth Century, CLXI (June, 1957), 583-585.
          The Entertainer has received more serious
     criticism than it deserves. The play only suc-
     ceeds on the "stunt" level by giving Laurence
     Olivier a vehicle for his performance.

43 MC CLAIN, JOHN. "Import Has Fire, Gleam and Glow."
     New York Journal-American (October 2, 1957).*
     Reprinted in New York Theatre Critics' Reviews,
     XVIII (October 7, 1957), 246
          Except for the resolution, Look Back in
     Anger is a brilliant play.

44 MANNES, MARYA. "A Question of Timing." Reporter,
        XVI (November 14, 1957), 38
            Look Back in Anger is part of a movement in
        contemporary theatre toward a revolt against
        deception and a promotion of the philosophy of
        "I stink, therefore I am."

45 MILLGATE, MICHAEL. "A Communication: A Good Word
        for England." Partisan Review, XXIV (Summer,
        1957), 428-431
            Look Back in Anger is among the signs of a
        new and hopeful movement away from hypocrisy
        and from institutional cultism and corruption.
        The play is viewed in terms of the contemporary
        British society and compared to other literary
        works felt to be pointing in the same direction.

46 _____. "An Uncertain Feeling in England." New
        Republic, CXXXVII (September 9, 1957), 16-17
            Comparison of Jimmy Porter in Osborne's Look
        Back in Anger with Jim Dixon in Amis' Lucky Jim
        and the works of other contemporaries.

47 "It's Done in a Rage." Newsweek, L (October 14,
        1957), 114
            Stresses the innovative nature of Look Back
        in Anger.

48 New York Times (April 10, 1957), p.37:3
            Osborne is divorced from Pamela.

48a "Anger." New York Times (October 13, 1957), VI,
        p.32:4
            Reprints selections from Jimmy Porter's
        "speeches" in Look Back in Anger to show what
        the angry young men "are all about."

49 "Good-Natured Man." New Yorker, XXXIII (October 26,
    1957), 36-37
        Brief article on Osborne two weeks after the
    Broadway opening of Look Back in Anger. Numer-
    ous quotes from Osborne on a comparison of
    American and British theatre and his reactions
    to America.

50 PANTER-DOWNES, MOLLIE. "Letter from London." New
    Yorker, XXXIII (September 28, 1957), 153-154
        The Entertainer is "an extremely poor play,"
    but in some ways is reminiscent of Noel Coward
    and Gertrude Lawrence.

51 RAYMOND, JOHN. "A Look Back at Mr. Osborne." New
    Statesman, LIII (January 16, 1957), 66-67
        Review of Look Back in Anger after its publi-
    cation in book form. Jimmy Porter and the
    other characters in the play have already become
    archetypal figures for their generation, but
    they express no message, no propaganda, and pre-
    sent the class struggle for what it is and
    their lives as they live them.

52 _____. "Mid-Century Blues." New Statesman, LIV
    (October 12, 1957), 464
        The Entertainer's major theme is the degen-
    eration of English society into "a mood of
    national impotence."

53 SCHLESINGER, ARTHUR. "Look Back in Amazement."
    New Republic, CXXXVII (December 23, 1957), 19-
    21. Reprinted in Schlesinger's The Politics of
    Hope.
        Look Back in Anger is not really about in-
    tellectual frustration or class conflict, but
    about Porter's lack of recognition that he is a

ABOUT JOHN OSBORNE (1957)   B56

SCHLESINGER, ARTHUR (cont.)
homosexual. The fascination of audiences for
the play is a result of the "prevalent obsession
of our theatre, if not our age:" homosexual
anxiety.

54 SCOTT, J. D. "Britain's Angry Young Men: A Gallery
of Lucky Jims." Saturday Review, XL (July 27,
1957), 8-11
Discusses the social change in England pro-
ducing educated young men who refuse to become
gentlemen. Indicative of this process are
Kingsley Amis' Lucky Jim and John Osborne's
Look Back in Anger. The development of the
angry young man is symptomatic of the pain involved with Britain's move toward social equal-
ity.

55 SCOTT-KILVERT, IAN. "The Hero in Search of a Dramatist: The Plays of John Osborne." Encounter,
IX (December, 1957), 26-30
Osborne revolutionized the English theatre by
being able to capture and hold an audience,
something that was not accomplished in the drama
directed toward the upper class. His plays are
a personal, not political, denunciation of what
is wrong in the English middle class society.
By sweeping away the normal conventions of
speech and behavior, Osborne creates a new type
of perception in the audience based on the un-
familiarity of the new manners. Osborne's primary deficiency is in being an actor; it results
in "retreating into a kind of professional
mystique and a world of essentially stagey in-
terests and values."

56 SMITH, MICHAEL. "Roads to Sanity?" Village Voice
(October 16, 1957), p.11

21

<u>B56</u>   ABOUT JOHN OSBORNE (1957)

SMITH, MICHAEL (cont.)
    Jimmy Porter is compared to Dean Moriarity
in Jack Kerouac's <u>On the Road</u>. The anguish of
both characters is "the direct result of a genu-
ine, all too clear-eyed recognition of where
they are and what and how small they have been
forced to become."

57 TALLMER, JERRY. "Look Forward to What?" <u>Village</u>
    <u>Voice</u> (October 16, 1957), pp.9-10
        The play sometimes appears ridiculous, some-
    times shocking, but "<u>Look Back in Anger</u> has
    this main virtue, it gets people talking."

58 "Angry and Active." <u>Theatre Arts</u>, XLI (December,
    1957), 11
        Osborne is an accomplished actor and this
    background is evident in the writing and pro-
    duction of his plays.

59 "Look Back in Anger." <u>Theatre Arts</u>, XLI (December,
    1957), 18
        A discussion of the play's ability to arouse
    emotion and a "critical box score" giving a
    selection of critical opinions on the play
    after its New York opening.

60 "The Most Angry Fella." <u>Time</u>, LXIX (April 22,
    1957), 90, 93
        Osborne's plays are little more than angry
    outbursts of his own troubled life. They are
    not great, nor even good plays--they merely
    give the "illusion of movement"--but his work
    can provide a mediocre vehicle which a great
    actor, such as Laurence Olivier, can turn into
    a superb theatrical event.

ABOUT JOHN OSBORNE (1957)   B65

61 "Lucky Jim and His Pals." Time, LXIX (May 27,
      1957), 106, 108, 111
          General review article on the major early
      publications of the figures in the angry young
      man movement. Osborne and Look Back in Anger
      are briefly mentioned, and Amis' Lucky Jim is
      seen to be the most notable work of the move-
      ment.

62 "New Plays in Manhattan." Time, LXX (October 14,
      1957), 85
          Includes comments on Look Back in Anger and
      its emotional appeal, biographical details on
      Osborne, and numerous quotes from him on differ-
      ent subjects. Osborne and his play are only
      superficially exciting, the stuff of intellec-
      tual and artistic shallowness.

63 TREWIN, J. C. "A Tale of Three Nights." Illus-
      trated London News, CCXXX (April 27, 1957), 702
          Considers the entire worth of The Entertainer
      to be Olivier's creation.

64 _____. "United Kingdom." World Theatre, VI
      (Summer, 1957), 158
          "Mr. Osborne is an over-praised, bitter dra-
      matist"; The Entertainer is unsuccessful; and
      Olivier gives "the best individual performance
      in a modern play."

65 _____. "The Latest Immortals." Illustrated London
      News, CCXXXI (September 28, 1957), 524
          Without Olivier's performance, The Enter-
      tainer would depict itself more as it really is,
      "cheaply conceived and shoddily written."

66 TYNAN, KENNETH. "A Whole of a Week." London Ob-
       server (April 4, 1957), p.13
           Although the character of Archie Rice is "one
       of the great acting parts of our age," the play
       is unsatisfactory because it attempts to do too
       much within its limited focus.

67 WAIN, JOHN. "The Entertainer." Listener, LVII
       (May 2, 1957), 711-712
           The production, direction, and acting com-
       bine with Osborne's strength and talent to make
       The Entertainer a "powerful experience," both
       dramatically successful and culturally intro-
       spective.

68 WATERMAN, ROLLENE. "Gallery of Lucky Jims." Satur-
       day Review, XL (July 27, 1957), 9
           Brief biographical details on Osborne, Amis,
       Wain, and Braine.

69 WATT, DAVID. "Coming Unstuck." Spectator, CXCVIII
       (April 19, 1957), 517
           The Entertainer is entertaining, but a
       "brilliant disappointment" because of the flat
       characters, lack of direction, and the shallow-
       ness of dialogue.

70 _____. "Class Report." Encore (September, 1957).*
       Reprinted in The Encore Reader.
           Although Look Back in Anger is a class con-
       scious work, it is most important because it
       created a new audience for British drama: "a
       small, lower middle-class intelligentsia whose
       frustrations and bayings were reflected in the
       play."

71 WATTS, RICHARD. "Impressive Drama of Angry Youth."
       New York Post (October 2, 1957).* Reprinted in

24

WATTS, RICHARD (cont.)
New York Theatre Critics' Reviews, XVIII (October 7, 1957), 244
Look Back in Anger is the best postwar British play. The central character differs from the earlier American protest hero because of his display of complete frustration and exasperating behavior and his general lack of concern for social or political aims.

72 WEBSTER, MARGARET. "A Look at the London Season."
Theatre Arts, XLI (May, 1957), 28
A short review of Look Back in Anger stressing the play's emotional and evocative power.

73 WORSLEY, T. C. "Minority Culture." New Statesman,
LII (January 26, 1957), 97-98
In Worsley's discussion of the Third Programme, he makes a passing reference to Osborne.

74 _____. "Cut and Come Again." New Statesman, LIII
(April 20, 1957), 512
Great praise for Laurence Olivier's portrayal of Archie Rice and Osborne's dialogue in The Entertainer, but complains that the playwright has not yet mastered basic dramatic techniques.

75 _____. "England, Our England." New Statesman, LIV
(September 21, 1957), 343-344
Points out many structural weaknesses in The Entertainer, which are primarily caused by Osborne's failure to get as far away as he would like from the well-made play.

76 WYATT, EUPHEMIA VAN RENSSELAER. "Theater." Catholic
World, CLXXXVI (December, 1957), 226
Unfavorable toward Look Back in Anger because it is so extreme.

JOHN OSBORNE: A REFERENCE GUIDE

AO   ABOUT JOHN OSBORNE (1958)

A. Books--1958

None

B. Articles--1958

1 ALLSOP, KENNETH. The Angry Decade. London: Peter
     Owen, 1958, pp.96-132
        Biographical criticism and a somewhat de-
     tailed analysis of Look Back in Anger and The
     Entertainer. Many references to the contempo-
     rary critical opinions of the plays and an em-
     phasis on the effect of Look Back in Anger on
     the British theatre.

2 ASTON, FRANK. "Sir Laurence Turns Hoofer." New
     York World-Telegram (February 13, 1958).* Re-
     printed in New York Theatre Critics' Reviews,
     XIX (February 17, 1958), 357
        After Look Back in Anger, it is a "surprise
     to see that The Entertainer is hard drama and
     high theatre that wrenches you with pity for
     the hopeless and the helpless."

3 _____. "George Dillon at the Golden." New York
     World-Telegram (November 5, 1958).* Reprinted
     in New York Theatre Critics' Reviews, XIX (No-
     vember 10, 1958), 219
        "The play demonstrated again the Osborne
     fixation on the kind of mind that seems nasty
     and mean, but is faintly touched with decency.
     Despite his preoccupation with the disgusting
     and defeatist, Mr. Osborne is actuated by com-
     passion."

4 ATKINSON, BROOKS. "Theatre: Olivier in The Enter-
     tainer." New York Times (February 13, 1958),
     p.22:2. Reprinted in New York Theatre Critics'

26

ATKINSON, BROOKS (cont.)
    <u>Reviews</u>, XIX (February 17, 1958), 360
        Although Laurence Olivier and Tony Richard-
son deserve praise, <u>The Entertainer</u> "is as tired
as the situation it portrays. The anger is per-
functory; the pathos is empty."

5   ____. "The Entertainer." <u>New York Times</u> (Febru-
    ary 25, 1958), II, p.1:1
        Praises Olivier's acting, but feels that
Osborne's writing fails because it is ineffec-
tual and uninteresting.

6   ____. "Theatre: <u>George Dillon</u>." <u>New York Times</u>
    (November 5, 1958), p.44:1. Reprinted in <u>New
York Theatre Critics' Reviews</u>, XIX (November
10, 1958), 221
        Compared with <u>Look Back in Anger</u>, this play
lacks vitality and a large scale focus. The
criticism of modern life is repeated so much
throughout <u>Epitaph for George Dillon</u> that it
becomes a rather "monotonous" play.

7   ____. "Two from Abroad." <u>New York Times</u> (Novem-
    ber 16, 1958), II, p.1:1
        <u>Epitaph for George Dillon</u> does not have the
power of <u>Look Back in Anger</u>. It "is written in
the slice-of-life technique of the old naturalistic drama; it does escape the misery of its
subject matter, and it does not exploit the
theater as an art form."

8 BARBER, JOHN. "Why Look Back Mr. Osborne?" <u>London
    Daily Express</u> (February 12, 1958), p.11
        <u>Epitaph for George Dillon</u> "is a lumpy, occa-
sionally vivid, often embarrassing affair--from
the desk of a born dramatist. But it is not a
good play."

9   BARBOUR, THOMAS. "Theatre Chronicle." Hudson Re-
        view, XI (Spring, 1958), 118-120
            Look Back in Anger is the breakthrough into a
        new age for British theatre. Osborne is obvi-
        ously influenced by American realistic drama,
        but his play is peculiarly English in the flu-
        ency of dialogue and the stress on character
        rather than plot. Because of the plot's insuf-
        ficiency and lack of "inevitable action," Os-
        borne is more of a "reporter" than an artist.

10 BEAUFORT, JOHN. "Second Play by Osborne Reaches
        U.S." Christian Science Monitor (February 24,
        1958), p.6
            At some times, Beaufort appears to praise
        Osborne for his social inquiry and writing, but
        ends this review with a statement on the degen-
        erate nature of The Entertainer's subject: "The
        notes are sour because the emotional strings
        are false."

11 BOOTH, JOHN. "Rebel Playwright." New York Times
        (November 2, 1958), II, p.3:1
            Discussion of Osborne's career and an inter-
        view after his success with Look Back in Anger
        and The Entertainer and prior to the New York
        opening of Epitaph for George Dillon. Osborne
        discusses his general ideas, refuses to go into
        detail on the meaning behind his plays, and
        admits that he has few "satisfactions" outside
        of his work.

12 BRIEN, ALAN. "Broken Mould." Spectator, CC (Febru-
        ary 21, 1958), 232
            Generally favorable review of Epitaph for
        George Dillon. In his first three plays Os-
        borne's major contribution to the modern theatre

'BRIEN, ALAN (cont.)
has been his "demonstration that failure is as
agonising and as dramatic for the third-rater
as for the genius."

13 CHAPMAN, JOHN. "Stunt Role as 'The Entertainer'
Makes a Great Dish for Olivier." New York
Daily News (February 13, 1958).* Reprinted in
New York Theatre Critics' Reviews, XIX (February 17, 1958), 359.
The Entertainer is presented as a series of
vaudeville sketches in fast succession and
overly emotionalized action. It is a "great"
vehicle for Olivier.

14 _____. "Epitaph for George Dillon: R.I.P." New
York Daily News (November 5, 1958).* Reprinted
in New York Theatre Critics' Reviews, XIX (November 10, 1958), 220
The play "is, to my foreign ear, dispiriting,
disheartening, disenchanted and discombobulated."

15 CHURCHILL, RANDOLPH. "Portrait of the Artist as an
Angry Young Gentleman." Encounter, X (January,
1958), 66-68
Written in response to Osborne's "And They
Call It Cricket." A scathing attack upon Osborne's ability to say anything intelligent or
of worth. Osborne and Kenneth Tynan are
branded as angry young men who have very little
to be angry about.

16 CLURMAN, HAROLD. "Theatre." Nation, CLXXXVI
(March 1, 1958), 192-193
The Entertainer is symptomatic of the degen-
eration and meaninglessness found in English
society, which accounts for the play's great

CLURMAN, HAROLD (cont.)
   popularity. But it is not a good play because
   of its poor symbolic construction and lack of
   direction. "The Entertainer is the immature
   work of a gifted, ambitious, battling young man."

17   ____. Lies Like Truth. New York: Macmillan,
        1958, 167, 190-192
           Reprints Clurman's review of Look Back in
        Anger from Nation.

18   COLEMAN, ROBERT. "Entertainer Proves Boring." New
        York Daily Mirror (February 13, 1958).* Re-
        printed in New York Theatre Critics' Reviews,
        XIX (February 17, 1958), 358
           The play is bitter, confusing, and boring--
        "a tasteless disappointment."

19   ____. "Epitaph for George Dillon Not to be
        Missed." New York Daily Mirror (November 5,
        1958).* Reprinted in New York Theatre Critics'
        Reviews, XIX (November 10, 1958), 220
           The play is a tremendous success because of
        its "brilliant theatrical writing." In Look
        Back in Anger and The Entertainer, Osborne has
        been carried away by the angry stature, but here
        he appears more willing to attempt an under-
        standing posture.

20   CORINA, LESLIE. "Still Looking Back." New Repub-
        lic, CXXXVIII (February 10, 1958), 22
           Attempts to refute Arthur Schlesinger's idea
        that Look Back in Anger's popularity arises
        from implicit homosexuality. Instead, at the
        root of the play's popularity is the class
        struggle and to some extent a desire to see
        something shocking on the stage.

21 DEMMING, BARBARA. "John Osborne's War Against the
    Philistines." Hudson Review, XI (Autumn, 1958),
    410-419
        Extensive criticism of Look Back in Anger and
    The Entertainer, which is motivated in large
    part by a response to Mary McCarthy's article
    "A New Word." The major point of contention is
    the reforming aspect of Osborne's work. Demming
    feels there is no room for Osborne's anger,
    which is only his own complacent snobbery, be-
    cause it is an intrusion in his drama.

22 DRIVER, TOM. "Earlier Osborne." Christian Century,
    LXXV (December 10, 1958), 1436
        Praises Epitaph for George Dillon as being a
    better play than Look Back in Anger or The En-
    tertainer. It mirrors and gives insight into
    the feelings of isolation and lack of identity
    in modern society.

23 DUPEE, F. W. "Isn't Life a Terrible Thing, Thank
    God." Partisan Review, XXV (Winter, 1958), 122-
    126. Reprinted in Dupee's "The King of the
    Cats" and Other Remarks on Writers and Writing
    under the title "England Now--Ariel or Caliban."
        Osborne's Look Back in Anger and Dylan
    Thomas' Under Milkwood are indicative of the
    "social stalemate" in contemporary Britain.

24 GIBBS, WOLCOTT. "The Dimmest View." New Yorker,
    XXXIV (February 22, 1958), 63
        The Entertainer is an extremely distressing
    but meaningless tragedy. The major problems
    are intolerable ideas coupled with a "grating"
    presentation. Praise for Olivier's perform-
    ance.

B25   ABOUT JOHN OSBORNE (1958)

25 GRAEF, HILDA. "Why All This Anger?" Catholic
      World, CLXXXVIII (November, 1958), 122-128
         Look Back in Anger expresses the essence of
      the angry young man movement, but the play,
      stripped of actors and stage, is really no more
      than a contemporary revival of the Cain story.

26 HATCH, ROBERT. "Theatre." Nation, CLXXXVII (Novem-
      ber 22, 1958), 394-395
         Epitaph for George Dillon is a vacuum of
      nothingness in which all of the characters come
      forth to tell us they are nothing and then re-
      main so throughout. The play "is not a dis-
      covery, it is a tautology."

27 _____. "Sir Archie Rice." Saturday Review, XLI
      (March 1, 1958), 24
         Archie Rice is a person that never pretends
      to be more than a bastard and recognizes the
      need for passion in a lukewarm world of medioc-
      rity. The structure of the play shifts from
      Archie's vaudeville stage to his home life. It
      is a pattern of an individual nightmare of
      fighting for existence. In all, The Entertainer
      is the "most perfect performance and most uncom-
      promisingly accurate observation of underlying
      human conflict yet achieved in the new genera-
      tion of theatre."

28 HEWES, HENRY. "The 'Cad' as Hero." Saturday Re-
      view, XLI (November 22, 1958), 24-25
         George Dillon is the first creation of the
      Osborne line of "cad" heroes that includes
      Jimmy Porter, Archie Rice, and Paul Slickey.
      The purpose of the main character in this play
      is to point to the hypocrisy that exists in so-
      ciety. While he and the rest of Osborne's
      heroes are not "nice people," they are at least
      honest to themselves.

29 HILTON, FRANK. "Britain's New Class." Encounter,
       X (February, 1958), 59-63
          Jimmy Porter is the violent response in the
       contemporary British theatre to the social
       self-criticism. His picture of the world is
       invented and the invention is based on the most
       worn out ideals of the social system, politics,
       and sex.

30 KERR, WALTER. "First Night Report: The Entertain-
       er." New York Herald-Tribune (February 13,
       1958), p.18. Reprinted in New York Theatre
       Critics' Reviews, XIX (February 17, 1958), 358
          Osborne has replaced the "revolutionary in-
       tellectuals of Look Back in Anger with a com-
       monplace chaos of near-illiterate deadbeats" in
       The Entertainer. The play is "truly moving"
       and Olivier's performance outstanding.

31 _____. "First Night Report: Epitaph for George
       Dillon." New York Herald-Tribune (November 5,
       1958), p.24. Reprinted in New York Theatre
       Critics' Reviews, XIX (November 10, 1958), 219
          The character of George Dillon only gains
       virtue when he is compared to the low state of
       those around him, but he is "committed to self-
       pity" and never reaches the quality of Jimmy
       Porter's outrage.

32 KITCHIN, LAURENCE. "Theatre--Nothing But Theatre."
       Encounter, X (April, 1958), 39
          Osborne's change in the scope of the theatre
       was made through conventional dramatic forms,
       forms which keep intruding throughout the per-
       formance because of his immaturity as a play-
       wright.

JOHN OSBORNE: A REFERENCE GUIDE

B33 ABOUT JOHN OSBORNE (1958)

33 LANGMAN, F. H. "The Generation That Got Lost Stay-
ing Home: A Letter to Jimmy Porter." Theoria,
XI (1958), 29–30
Interesting response to Look Back in Anger
in the form of an open letter to Jimmy Porter
in which Langman concludes that Porter's anger
is produced by his own infantile selfishness.
The letter is followed by an "editorial post-
script" which compares Porter with the decay
found in all of the productions by the angry
young men, especially those of Beckett and
Braine.

34 LARDNER, JOHN. "The Theatre: An Artist and a
Sadist." New Yorker, XXXIV (November 15, 1958),
101–103
Dillon is a thoroughly disgusting character.
However, Osborne and Creighton look at him as a
thoroughly honest character and an example of a
universal tragedy of modern man.

35 LEWIS, THEOPHILUS. "Theatre." America, XCVIII
(March 22, 1958), 736
Unfavorable review of The Entertainer. Lewis
is becoming tired of Osborne's "crybaby" drama.

36 _____. "Theatre." America, C (November 29, 1958),
299
"It is dramatically satisfying when Dillon's
success turns to ashes."

37 "Olivier on the Seamy Side." Life, XLIV (March 10,
1958), 118
Osborne is "shockingly real" and Olivier depicts "electrifying showmanship" in The Entertainer.

34

38 "Royal Court Theatre." London Times (February 12,
        1958), p.3e
            The play possesses many of the elements of
        Look Back in Anger. The strong central charac-
        ter of Dillon is perhaps better drawn than the
        character of Jimmy Porter. At times, relief is
        needed in the over-presentation of decadence.

39 "Putting Drama in Touch With Contemporary Life: Two
        Years of the English Stage Company." London
        Times (March 19, 1958), p.3b
            Osborne, Look Back in Anger, and The Enter-
        tainer are discussed in this history of the
        first two years of the English Stage Company.

40 "French Approve of the Angry Young Man." London
        Times (April 25, 1958), p.3e
            Quotes some praising French critical reviews
        of Angry Young Man, the French title of Look
        Back in Anger.

41 "Stage Censorship Reform." London Times (May 2,
        1958), p.6e
            Osborne noted as one of those supporting the
        censorship reform.

42 "Revised Version of George Dillon." London Times
        (May 30, 1958), p.16e
            The title of the play is shortened to George
        Dillon and some of the dialogue is retouched.
        The play has "obvious affinities" with
        Osborne's later work, especially Look Back in
        Anger.

43 "Look Back in Anger." London Times (June 28, 1958),
        p.10e
            Notice that Tony Richardson will direct the
        film of Look Back in Anger and also mentions a

35

B43   ABOUT JOHN OSBORNE (1958)

"Look Back in Anger" (cont.)
     number of literary works from the angry young
     man movement that are currently being filmed.

44 London Times (July 21, 1958), p.12g
         Notice that Look Back in Anger will be made
     into a film.

45 "Theatrical Illusion and Human Illusions." London
         Times Literary Supplement (October 31, 1958),
         p.620
             Epitaph for George Dillon deals with man's
         illusions about his own capacities.

46 "Theatrical Illusion and Human Intelligence." Lon-
         don Times Literary Supplement (October 31, 1958)
         p.620
             Review of the published version of Epitaph
         for George Dillon. This play is more soundly
         constructed than Look Back in Anger and The En-
         tertainer, and the major character is more sym-
         pathetic than Jimmy Porter and Archie Rice.

47 MC CARTHY, MARY. "A New Word." Harper's Bazaar
         (April, 1958), pp.176-178
             Jimmy Porter declares war on the stasis of
         modern existence and is a "calculated irritant"
         that prevents the other people in Look Back in
         Anger from succumbing to this stasis. The only
         virtue that is real for him is the "working
         class virtue." Shaw and Heartbreak House are
         compared biographically and thematically to Os-
         borne and The Entertainer. Osborne is primarily
         a social critic who names modern society, its
         evil and oppression of the individual, a "new
         word": hell.

48 MC CLAIN, JOHN. "Sir Larry Romps in Strong Vehicle."
    New York Journal-American (February 13, 1958).*
    Reprinted in New York Theatre Critics' Reviews,
    XIX (February 17, 1958), 359
        The Entertainer is "magical theater, super-
    latively performed."

49 _____. "A Well-Acted Play." New York Journal-
    American (November 5, 1958).* Reprinted in New
    York Theatre Critics' Reviews, XIX (November 10,
    1958), 222
        Although Epitaph for George Dillon is com-
    pelling and Osborne and Creighton write extreme-
    ly well about an intricate emotional life, the
    play is unsuccessful because of its "extreme
    verbiage."

50 MANNES, MARYA. "The Player's the Thing." The Re-
    porter, XVIII (March 20, 1958), 39
        Like Look Back in Anger, the thought in this
    play is unclear and the invective has even less
    motivation. At least, in the earlier play the
    characters were interesting because they were
    different, but in The Entertainer the newness
    passes. The only good thing about this play is
    Olivier's great performance.

51 MORGAN, EDWIN. "That Uncertain Feeling." Encore,
    (May, 1958).* Reprinted in The Encore Reader.
        Comparative discussion of Osborne, Williams,
    and Miller. Osborne's plays succeed in arous-
    ing the audience's emotions, but tend to fail
    in lack of thematic depth.

52 "Correspondence." New Republic, CXXXVIII (January
    20, 1958), 23-24
        Two responses by Murray Brown and Aaron Levy
    to Arthur Schlesinger's review of Look Back in

B52   ABOUT JOHN OSBORNE (1958)

"Correspondence." (cont.)
    Anger. Brown restates the social protest inter-
    pretation; Levy offers an explanation of
    Porter's anger as a "neurotic response."

53 "New Play in London." New York Times (February 12,
        1958), p.33:8
            Briefly discusses the history and London re-
        ception of Epitaph for George Dillon.

54 "Epitaph Makes Ad Appeal." New York Times (Novem-
        ber 17, 1958), p.38:3
            Because of lagging ticket sales, the produ-
        cers of the play created an advertising campaign
        offering audiences their money back if they did
        not like the play.

55 "On a Rowdy Adventure." Newsweek, LI (February 24,
        1958), 62
            The degeneration of the Rice family and
        vaudeville entertainment in The Entertainer
        symbolizes the decline of England.

56 "Talk With the Playwright." Newsweek, LI (February
        24, 1958), 62
            Osborne's comments on acting, Hollywood, the
        Broadway theatre, and his critics.

57 "The 'Hero' is a Heel." Newsweek, LII (November 17,
        1958), 75
            Epitaph for George Dillon is "Tough going
        but required sociology for theatre goers."

58 POPKIN, HENRY. "Theatre II." Kenyon Review, XX
        (Spring, 1958), 309-310
            Look Back in Anger offers no hope for a solu-
        tion to the problems it presents, neither
        through socialism as in some contemporary dramas
        nor through love as in West Side Story.

59 ROLO, CHARLES. "A Certain Snarl." Atlantic, CCI
       (March, 1958), 100
           The Entertainer produces a feeling of irrita-
       tion and seems to say that the only "genuine"
       people in England are among the working class,
       but also they are apparently a most self-pity-
       ing lot. Osborne's main declaration "to date
       is the size of the chip on his shoulder."

60 SHIPLEY, JOSEPH T. "Five Performances in Uneven
       Plays." New Leader, XLI (November 17, 1958),
       28
           Epitaph for George Dillon "is unable to make
       us believe that anyone in it is worth caring
       about."

61 SMITH, MICHAEL. "Theatre: Look Back in Anger."
       Village Voice (November 12, 1958), p.7
           In the revival of Look Back in Anger, the
       play is still seen as a "stimulating evening's
       entertainment," but "we are no longer blinded
       to the play's faults."

62 SPENDER, STEPHEN. "London Letter: Anglo-Saxon Atti-
       tudes." Partisan Review, XXV (Winter, 1958),
       110-116
           John Osborne is much like Dylan Thomas. Not
       only are they both always "different," but
       Osborne is close to Thomas philosophically.
       Osborne shows that man has lost love for his
       neighbor by gaining pride that we all belong to
       a just modern social state. He is seen as an
       advanced critical appraiser of society.

63 _____. "From a Diary." Encounter, XI (December,
       1958), 75-77
           Spender's view of Osborne's social criticism
       from a Warsaw vantage point. The Entertainer

_____. (cont.)
in Poland is like a play with characters who
complain of headaches, performed for cancer pa-
tients. In relation to the "real evils" of the
world (the concentration camps, Communism),
Osborne's type of protest drama is a facade.

64 SUNDRANN, JEAN. "The Necessary Illusion." Antioch
Review, XVIII (Summer, 1958), 236-244
Discusses the failure of Americans to recognize the ideas expressed in contemporary English literature. The Entertainer is used as
the primary example; its major theme is the
conflict of the old with the new. The expres-
sions of the angry young men are of "the lost
identity of the past" and the development of a
new identity. Archie Rice shows the past con-
fronting the present and the resulting inability
to act when he is psychologically dead.

65 TALLMER, JERRY. "Homage to Some Entertainers."
Village Voice (March 12, 1958), pp.7-8
The Entertainer is an unforgettable play
with a great performance by Olivier. This play
helps give further appreciation to Osborne's
growing maturity as a dramatist.

66 _____. "Theatre Uptown." Village Voice (November
12, 1958), pp.7-8
Epitaph for George Dillon is less satisfying
than Look Back in Anger or The Entertainer, but
still it is dramatically powerful and incisive
in its character study of Dillon.

67 Theatre Arts, XLII (April, 1958), 22-23
Praises Olivier's performance, but finds The
Entertainer "only intermittently brilliant,
rather garish and decidedly chilly."

68 "New Plays in Manhattan." Time, LXXI (February 24,
    1958), 52
        Praises The Entertainer and compares it to
    Look Back in Anger on several points. Includes
    comments from Laurence Olivier on Osborne and
    the play.

69 _____. Time, LXXII (November 17, 1958), 62
        "There is the feebleness of something dead-
    ended in the author's writing" in Epitaph for
    George Dillon.

70 TYNAN, KENNETH. "A Phony or a Genius?" London
    Observer (February 16, 1958), p.12. Reprinted
    in Tynan's Tynan on Theatre and Curtains.
        Epitaph for George Dillon is powerful and
    presents a unique picture of an artist dealing
    with neurosis and society. But the lack of a
    distinct conclusion on whether Dillon is a
    "good or bad" artist causes a final dissatis-
    faction. "Yet the fire is there, boiling and
    licking, however neurotically."

71 _____. "Men of Anger." Holiday, XXIII (April,
    1958), 92-93, 177, 179, 181-182, 184. Reprinted
    in Tynan's Tynan on Theatre under the title
    "The Angry Young Movement."
        A general discussion of the angry young man
    movement, but the primary focus throughout is
    on Osborne. In his comments on the effect of
    Look Back in Anger and The Entertainer, Tynan
    also refers to the social conditions from which
    they emerged. "Britain's angry young men may
    be jejune and strident, but they are involved
    in the only belief that matters: that life be-
    gins tomorrow."

72   WATTS, RICHARD.   "The Brilliance of Laurence
        Olivier."   New York Post (February 13, 1958).*
        Reprinted in New York Theatre Critics' Reviews,
        XIX (February 17, 1958), 360
            The Entertainer is at times unsatisfactory,
        but there is no doubt that Osborne is a
        talented dramatist "with a fresh and interest-
        ind mind."

73   _____.   "Brilliant Portrait of a Failure."   New
        York Post (November 5, 1958).* Reprinted in
        New York Theatre Critics' Reviews, XIX (Novem-
        ber 10, 1958), 221
            Epitaph for George Dillon "marks a definite
        advance for the author." It combines Osborne's
        skill in writing with his insight into the
        British social condition in a new, more de-
        tached fashion.

74   WYATT, EUPHEMIA VAN RENSSELAER.   "Theater."   Catho-
        lic World, CLXXXVII (April, 1958), 68
            "The Entertainer is by no means entertain-
        ment, no it is very absorbing drama."

75   WYATT, WOODROW.   Distinguished for Talent.   London:
        Hutchinson, 1958, 116–122
            Interesting biographical comment on Osborne
        based on Wyatt's interview with the author.
        With a background in the social circumstances
        surrounding Osborne and Look Back in Anger,
        Wyatt discusses the playwright's attempt to
        form a bridge of communication and a sense of
        value for the modern generation.

76 ZOLOTOW, SAM. "Dallas Hit Play to be Seen Here."
    New York Times (November 19, 1958), p.43:2
        Notice of the withdrawal of Epitaph for
    George Dillon and comments that only two custo-
    mers asked for their money back.

A. Books--1959

None

B. Articles--1959

1 ALVAREZ, A. "Anti-Establishment Drama." Partisan
    Review, XXVI (Fall, 1959), 606-611
        Deals in a general manner with the change in
    British drama after World War II and especially
    with the works of Osborne, Delaney, Behan, and
    Wesker. Their themes are seen to be aroused
    more from irritation, than by enthusiasm or
    causes. This irritation is shown through a
    specific technical form: total realism. This
    form is their main strength because of its
    immediate impact.

2 BALAKIAN, NONA. "The Flight From Innocence."
    Books Abroad, XXXIII (Summer, 1959), 260-270
        General essay on the new, angry writers in
    Britain. Includes brief comments on Osborne,
    Kingsley Amis, Iris Murdoch, John Wain, J. P.
    Donleavy, and John Braine.

3 BANHAM, REYNER. "1959 and All That." New States-
    man, LVII (May 16, 1959), 684
        Osborne's The World of Paul Slickey has re-
    ceived almost universal criticism for being

BANHAM, REYNER (cont.)
dull. The play is not dull, but it does have
almost every other fault (a list of the eight
major faults is conveniently provided).

4   BODE, CARL. "Redbrick Cinder(ella)?" College English, XX (April, 1959), 331-337
Osborne's Jimmy Porter is the progenitor of
the angry young man syndrome. Moving the
audience in a positive fashion is the primary
strength of the angry theme in Look Back in
Anger, The Entertainer, and Epitaph for George
Dillon.

5   BRIEN, ALAN. "No Epitaph For Osborne." Spectator,
CCII (May 15, 1959), 693-694
Osborne's The World of Paul Slickey is an
open challenge to the established society,
especially to the establishment of critics, and
thereby when the challenge is met by critical
denunciation it is only to be expected. The
play itself is funny and entertaining and
possesses all of Osborne's characteristic
faults and achievements.

6   _____. "Theatre London." Theatre Arts, XLIII (December, 1959), 20
In his first three plays, Osborne analyzed
the world of the failure (his own world), but
in The World of Paul Slickey the focus shifts
to a life characterized by achievement (a
change caused by Osborne's success). Although
there were many problems that caused the play
to fail, his "first musical was a courageous,
provocative, characteristically Osbornian ges-
ture that shook London's theatre like a one-man
earthquake."

7 BRUSTEIN, ROBERT. "Theatre Chronicle." Hudson Re-
      view, XII (Spring, 1959), 98-101
         The original Epitaph for George Dillon, co-
      authored by Osborne and Anthony Creighton, was
      revised and effectively made into an entirely
      new play by Osborne prior to its production.
      The play is evidence of Osborne's continuing
      maturation as a dramatist and, also, bears a
      close resemblance to George Orwell's Keep the
      Aspidistra Flying. Orwell is Osborne's adopted
      philosophical godfather.

8 CLURMAN, HAROLD. "The World of John Osborne."
      London Observer (May 10, 1959), p.23
         In The World of Paul Slickey, "Osborne has
      been his own worst enemy. Self loathing
      appears to be a driving force of his art. He
      should control it: he is not as bad as he
      thinks." The play at least shows how not to
      write a musical play.

9 DYSON, A. E. "Look Back in Anger." Critical Quar-
      terly, I (Winter, 1959), 318-326. Reprinted in
      Modern British Dramatists.
         A discussion of the "angry young man" myth
      that arose because of Look Back in Anger. Ex-
      tensive criticism of Jimmy Porter as the tor-
      mented modern man and the conditions that
      caused his situation. Osborne is praised for
      showing what the moral misfits, who are either
      martyred or praised for the wrong reasons, are
      really like.

JOHN OSBORNE: A REFERENCE GUIDE

10 FINDLATER, RICHARD. The Future of the Theatre.
     London: The Fabian Society, 1959
        Discusses the major problems (mainly eco-
     nomic) and possibilities of the British theatre
     during the postwar period and entering into the
     1960's.

11 GELB, ARTHUR. "Goldilocks Ends Run Here Feb. 28."
     New York Times (February 21, 1959), p.25:1
        Notice of the withdrawal of Epitaph for
     George Dillon.

12 HICKEY, WILLIAM. "John Osborne and the Thousand
     Undertakers." London Daily Express (May 6,
     1959), p.3
        Details regarding the audience and its reac-
     tion to the opening performance of The World of
     Paul Slickey.

13 KAUFFMANN, STANLEY. "Look Back at Osborne." New
     Republic, CXLI (September 28, 1959), 30-32
        Review of the movie Look Back in Anger.
     Osborne has written one long whining complaint
     on the hopelessness of modern man. The play is
     existentialism said with sophomoric terms and
     is the result of an incomplete understanding of
     the philosophical and social views of its time.
     Osborne has the possibility of becoming a dan-
     gerous distorter.

14 LANDSTONE, CHARLES. "From John Osborne to Shelagh
     Delaney." World Theatre, VIII (Autumn, 1959),
     203-216
        A general discussion of the English theatre
     during the 1950's and specifically concerning
     the breakthrough into the new theatrical style
     signified by Osborne's Look Back in Anger. The

LANDSTONE, CHARLES (cont.)
> major reason for the play's popular success was
> the reviews of its first production by Kenneth
> Tynan, the "prophet" of the new angry movement.

15 "Libel on Mr. Osborne in Daily Mail." London Times
> (February 19, 1959), p.7f
> > Osborne's suit against the Daily Mail for
> > calling him "the original Teddy Boy."

16 "Mr. Osborne's Musical Play." London Times (Febru-
> ary 27, 1959), p.6b
> > Notice of the rehearsals and the cast for
> > The World of Paul Slickey.

17 "Mr. Osborne's Musical Withdrawn." London Times
> (June 15, 1959), p.32
> > Notice that The World of Paul Slickey gave
> > its last performance on June 13, 1959.

18 "Theatre Folk in 'Ban the Bomb' Stroll." London
> Times (September 14, 1959), p.7d
> > Osborne's participation in picketing White-
> > hall in support of the Campaign for Nuclear
> > Disarmament.

19 "Bobby Howes in The Entertainer." London Times
> (October 20, 1959), p.4a
> > This play is the best evidence that Os-
> > borne's drama survives its contemporary situa-
> > tion and is of more than just "modish" interest.

20 MC CARTHY, MARY. "Odd Man In." Partisan Review,
> XXVI (Winter, 1959), 100-106
> > Dillon and his "phony" artist world are com-
> > pared to the chief characters in Eugene O'Neill's
> > A Touch of the Poet and Jean Genet's Deathwatch.

B21   ABOUT JOHN OSBORNE (1959)

21   _____. Sights and Spectacles. London: Heinemann,
       1959, 184-196
            Look Back in Anger "almost asks to be misun-
       derstood, like an infuriated wounded person;
       out of bravado, it coldly refuses to justify
       itself."

22   MANNES, MARYA. "The Fly in the Ointment."
       Reporter, XX (January 8, 1959), 36
            Brief, but complete, praise for Epitaph for
       George Dillon.

23   "Play by Osborne Creates a Storm." New York Times
       (May 6, 1959), p.48:7
            Discusses the critical reaction to the Lon-
       don opening of The World of Paul Slickey and
       its major points of satire.

24   New York Times (May 8, 1959), p.23:6
            Quotes two of Osborne's comments on the
       critics' reaction to The World of Paul Slickey.

25   "Osborne Musical Closes." New York Times (June 14,
       1959), p.32:3
            Notes the withdrawal of The World of Paul
       Slickey in London.

26   "The Observer Profile: John Osborne." London
       Observer (May 17, 1959), p.10
            General remarks on Osborne's dramatic career,
       socialist political views, ideas on authors and
       publicity, and his rebellious personality.

27   Theatre Arts, XLIII (January 1959), 21-23.
            Epitaph for George Dillon is a disconnected
       series of parts with no central unity. This
       fault makes it closer to The Entertainer than to

Theatre Arts (cont.)
Look Back in Anger. Its failure is not merely
a matter of an early stage of development in
Osborne's drama.

28 THOMPSON, JOHN. "Such Tired Jokes, Such Poor Aim,
Mr. Osborne!" London Daily Express (May 6,
1959), p.9
The play might be subtitled "'Osborne's
Folly'" since every element in the play turns
out to contribute to its total failure.

29 "Slickey's Slicker." Time, LXXIII (May 18, 1959),
48
Primarily concerns David Pelham's efforts to
save the play from financial disaster after its
critical rejection by the press.

30 TREWIN, J. C. "The World of the Theatre." Illustrated London News, CCXXXIV (May 16, 1959), 852
Brief comments on the play's faults and a
paragraph denouncing nihilism and anger in contemporary literature.

31 WILSON, A. "New Playwrights." Partisan Review,
XXV (Fall, 1959), 631-634
Mentions Osborne within the context of the
general aspect of the contemporary British
theatre.

AO   ABOUT JOHN OSBORNE (1960)

A. Books--1960

None

B. Articles--1960

1 DUNCAN, RONALD. "A Preface to the Sixties." Lon-
      don Magazine, VII (July, 1960), 15-19
         Although in 1956, Look Back in Anger looked
      startingly revolutionary, it really originated
      nothing beyond what Ibsen and Shaw had already
      accomplished.

2 FINDLATER, RICHARD. "The Case of Paul Slickey."
      Twentieth Century, CLXVII (1960), 29-38
         The World of Paul Slickey is a "bungled and
      boring" play, but the failure is perhaps neces-
      sary for Osborne's career.

3 FORSTER, PETER. "Not for Children." Spectator,
      CCV (November 11, 1960), 734
         A Subject of Scandal and Concern is dull,
      the directing poor, and the BBC time slot dis-
      appointing.

4 GASSNER, JOHN. Theatre at the Crossroads. New
      York: Holt, Rinehart and Winston, 1960, 175-177
         Brief chronicles on Osborne's Look Back in
      Anger and Epitaph for George Dillon.

5 KITCHIN, LAURENCE. Mid-Century Drama. London:
      Faber and Faber, 1960. Comments on Osborne re-
      printed in John Osborne: LOOK BACK IN ANGER, A
      Casebook.
         Brief mention of Osborne as the central
      figure in the English theatre's breakthrough
      into realistic drama. Kitchin relates the his-
      tory of Look Back in Anger's acceptance by the

50

KITCHIN, LAURENCE (cont.)
   Royal Court Theatre and comments that the two
   dramatic virtues in Osborne's work are his dic-
   tion and compassion in dealing with characters.

6 "First Television Play by Mr. Osborne." London
      Times (October 25, 1960), p.14e
         Notice of the scheduled time on BBC (November
      6, 1960) for A Subject of Scandal and Concern.

7 "A Subject of Scandal and Concern." London Times
      (November 7, 1960), p.16e
         Criticizes the school-like presentation of
      the play on the BBC.

8 MILNE, TOM. "The Hidden Face of Violence." Encore,
      VII (1960), 14-20. Reprinted in Modern British
      Dramatists and The Encore Reader.
         Look Back in Anger is a middle step between
      the theatre of Eliot and Fry and the theatre of
      Whiting, Pinter, and Arden. The indictment of
      man as a "dead soul" exists in his work, but
      people find his plays acceptable because they
      can channel their vision into areas of sex, mis-
      treatment of a wife, and violence. The indict-
      ment of man in Whiting, Pinter, and Arden exists
      without these channels.

9 SHERRY, RUTH FORBES. "Angry Young Men." Trace
      (May-June, 1960), pp.33-37
         Little more than a mention of Osborne in this
      running series of random comments on the angry
      young man movement.

10 TAUBMAN, HOWARD. "Theatre: Dillon Reborn." New
      York Times (December 29, 1960), p.17:1
         The play is indicative of the frustration and
      outrage felt by an entire generation of authors

B10   ABOUT JOHN OSBORNE (1960)

   TAUBMAN, HOWARD (cont.)
      and is an example of Osborne's compassion for
      the lower classes. The occasion for this re-
      view was an off-Broadway production of Epitaph
      for George Dillon.

11 THOMAS, JAMES. "This Osborne Piece Wasn't Worth the
      Fuss." London Daily Express (November 7, 1960),
      p.8
         A Subject of Scandal and Concern is a total
      failure. It is more of a "slow documentary"
      than a play.

12 TRILLING, OSSIA. "The Young British Drama." Modern
      Drama, III (September, 1960), 168-177
         General survey of the major events in con-
      temporary British drama. Osborne appears to be
      almost the philosophical father for the one-
      hundred and twenty playwrights writing in 1960
      and the best indication of the insecurity of
      playwrights in their finances, success, and
      social function.

13 WEISS, SAMUEL. "Osborne's Angry Young Play." Edu-
      cational Theatre Journal, XII (December, 1960),
      285-288
         Look Back in Anger signalled a revitalization
      of the English theatre. Osborne accomplishes
      firm social criticism within the "old lines" of
      realism without succumbing to "artificial 'pro-
      letarian' art." Osborne's major achievement is
      his probing of the psychosexual relationships
      between Jimmy and Alison Porter and his revela-
      tion of the social determinants.

ABOUT JOHN OSBORNE (1961)   B4

A. Books--1961

None

B. Articles--1961

1 ANDERSON, LINDSAY. "Stand Up! Stand Up!" Sight and
        Sound (Autumn, 1961), pp.10-13
            Views Look Back in Anger as "primarily the
        study of a temperament" among the young that re-
        volts against a social system based on a rela-
        tivistic moral vacuum.

2 BAILEY, SHIRLEY JEAN. "John Osborne: A Bibliogra-
        phy." Twentieth Century Literature, VII (1961),
        118-120.
            Checklist of Osborne's major writings and
        critical essays and reviews on his drama. In-
        cludes material published from 1956 through the
        third quarter of 1960.

3 BALLIET, WHITNEY. "Once More, With Feeling." New
        Yorker, XXXVI (January 14, 1961), 68, 70, 72
            Reviews the Actors Playhouse revival of Epi-
        taph for George Dillon.

4 DENNIS, NIGEL. "Out of the Box." Encounter, XVII
        (August, 1961), 51-53
            Luther and Brecht's Galileo are seen as the
        revival of the historical drama and an escape
        from the anticipated degeneration of the theatre
        due to Beckett and the absurdists. There is a
        brief notation of the historical antecedents of
        the historical drama, particularly with atten-
        tion to the Elizabethan stage. Luther's form is
        compared to the film, novel and epic because of
        its panoramic scope.

53

5   DENTY, VERA D. "The Psychology of Martin Luther."
    Catholic World, CXCIV (November, 1961), 99-105
        Very favorable toward Osborne's handling of
    the character study of Luther and of the entire
    play. Luther's only real fault is that it does
    not do "full justice to the man."

6   GASCOIGNE, BAMBER. "First Parson Singular." Spec-
    tator, CCVII (August 4, 1961), 171
        Very favorable review of Luther. The play
    depends on the focus on the individual and how a
    time of crisis produces demonstrable character
    changes. Osborne is praised as the greatest
    prose writer in the contemporary English theatre.

7   HALL, STUART. "Beyond Naturalism Pure." Encore,
    (November, 1961).* Reprinted in The Encore
    Reader.
        Compares Wesker's and Osborne's successes
    with the development of the modern naturalistic
    hero and ends with some comments on Arden. Os-
    borne's themes in Look Back in Anger and Luther
    find their most direct expression in The Enter-
    tainer, "where Osborne finds both the properly
    seedy hero and the representatively public sym-
    bol in the failed artist and the declining art
    of the music hall."

8   HOBSON, HAROLD. "Osborne's Distressing View of
    Luther." Christian Science Monitor (July 15,
    1961), p.4
        Luther is perhaps better than many by
    Brecht. It is not in any sense presenting a
    "comprehension of Christian values," but is a
    Marxist view of both Catholicism and Protestant-
    ism.

9   _____ . "Luther at Royal Court." Christian Science
        Monitor (August 5, 1961), p.12
            The play makes too much out of Luther's physi-
        cal problems. Luther is indicative of the con-
        temporary anti-religious attitude on the stage.

10   HUNTER, G. K. "The World of John Osborne." Criti-
        cal Quarterly, III (Spring, 1961), 76-81
            The major theme in Osborne's work is the con-
        flict of individual freedom and social re-
        straint. His first three plays are a progres-
        sion of these themes in different modes of pre-
        sentation. The World of Paul Slickey is a par-
        tial failure because it does not give enough
        scope for society as the background for Os-
        borne's presentation of ideas.

11   KING, SETH S. "Britain Damned by John Osborne."
        New York Times, (August 19, 1961), p.4:1
            Discussion of Osborne's open letter to the
        British people, "a letter of hate." Some pos-
        sible motivations for the letter, the protests
        in his plays, and his ideas on nuclear weapons
        are commented upon.

12   "Paris Premiere of Mr. Osborne's Luther." London
        Times (July 7, 1961), p.15a
            Luther is not a historical play, but a char-
        acter analysis in terms of the contemporary
        sensibility. Luther is changed from a revolu-
        tionary to a more domestic individual after the
        revolution has been won and his anger abated.
        Although the character study is intense, Osborne
        stops before he takes on any broader social
        issues.

B13   ABOUT JOHN OSBORNE (1961)

13 "Best Guarantee Yet of Mr. Osborne's Stamina." <u>London Times</u> (July 28, 1961), p.13a
      <u>Luther</u> marks a shift in Osborne's focus from a study of angry and frustrated failure to an analysis of a strong man "who draws from continual fierce diggings into the depths of self the strength to become the wedge to split Christendom."

14 "Court Theatre Chooses Its Plays for a Year." <u>London Times</u> (November 17, 1961), p.17c
      <u>The Blood of the Bamburgs</u> is chosen.

15 MANDER, JOHN. <u>The Writer and Commitment</u>. London: Secker and Warburg, 1961, 179–211
      Jimmy Porter's invective fails to say anything about society, because <u>Look Back in Anger</u> fails as a drama. The content of the play is only the view of Porter, and he is "unqualified and undefined" because of Osborne's failure to present well-drawn minor characters. Osborne, disregarding any biographical evidence, commits himself to the protagonist's view because no others are presented.

16 MILNE, TOM. "<u>Luther</u> and <u>The Devils</u>." <u>New Left Review</u>, XII (November–December, 1961), 55–57
      A general discussion of the use of historical settings in the contemporary theatre, especially in regard to Osborne's <u>Luther</u> and John Whiting's <u>The Devils</u>, and refutes the widely held contention that because of the introduction of the Brechtian historical mode modern drama is moving in the proper direction. The historicism of <u>Luther</u> tends to muffle the protest theme, confuse it, and give it an unnecessary ambiguity.

17 "Angriest Young Man." New York Times (August 19,
        1961), p.4:2
            Biographical article attempting to give some
        background for Osborne's anger with English
        society. Discusses his plays, their social
        themes, and his personality.

18 "John Osborne Seeks Divorce." New York Times (Octo-
        ber 4, 1961), p.18:3
            Osborne files for a divorce from Mary Ure.

19 PANTER-DOWNES, MOLLIE. "Letter from London." New
        Yorker, XXXVII (October 14, 1961), 200-201
            Praises Luther for its dialogue and the char-
        acterization of Luther's revolutionary image.

20 PRITCHETT, V. S. "Operation Osborne." New States-
        man, LXII (August 4, 1961), 163-164
            In contemporary historical drama, Brecht,
        Anouilh and others create, but Osborne only ex-
        pounds the known. Ambiguity of character, lack
        of organization, and a lifeless nature cause
        Luther to fail.

21 PRYCE-JONES, ALAN. "At the Theatre." Theatre Arts,
        XLV (March, 1961), 68
            Short review criticizing the lack of a clear
        social milieu in Epitaph for George Dillon.

22 ROSSELLI, J. "At Home With Lucifer." Reporter, XXV
        (October 12, 1961), 50
            This play is evidence of Osborne's broadening
        scope of talent and interest. He is now "able
        to make his rebel spurt out passion and yet to
        see him from the outside." Although lapses
        occur, Luther is Osborne's most coherent and
        well developed play.

B23   ABOUT JOHN OSBORNE (1961)

23 "Angry Young Luther." Time, LXXVII (June 30, 1961),
    58-59
        The character of Luther is the Jimmy Porter of
    the Reformation. Osborne fails to draw his
    modern parallels and reduces Luther's actions to
    scatology.

24 TREWIN, J. C. "A Word in the Ear." Illustrated
    London News, CCIXL (August 12, 1961), 266
        Luther minimizes a great historical figure,
    sacrifices dialogue for invective, and generally
    is a replay of "the old cult of uglification."

25 TYNAN, KENNETH. Curtains. New York: Atheneum,
    1961, 130-2, 173-176, 205-207. Reprints Tynan's
    reviews from the London Observer of Look Back in
    Anger, The Entertainer, and Epitaph for George
    Dillon.

26 WHITING, JOHN. "Luther." London Magazine, I (Octo-
    ber, 1961), 57-59. Reprinted in Whiting's On
    Theatre.
        General summary of Osborne's career to the
    production of Luther. The change in Osborne,
    from letting his characters speak in his first
    three plays to what now appears to be Osborne
    himself on the stage, is the most noticeable
    difference. The change culminates in Luther,
    where the billboard could easily read "'John
    Osborne by Luther.'"

27 WILLIAMS, RAYMOND. "The New English Drama." Twen-
    tieth Century, CLXX (1961), 169-180. Reprinted
    in Modern British Dramatists.
        General article on British drama during the
    twentieth century stressing the major innova-
    tions.

John Osborne: A Reference Guide

ABOUT JOHN OSBORNE (1961)   B3

28 ZOLOTOW, SAM. "Luther Dropped at Italian Fete."
New York Times (April 4, 1961), p.41
Luther is withdrawn from Gian Carlo Minotti's
Festival of Two Worlds "because of its theme."

A. Books--1962

None

B. Articles--1962

1 BARNES, CLIVE. "I Could Hardly Stay Awake." London
Daily Express (July 20, 1962), p.4
Under Plain Cover and The Blood of the Bam-
burgs are both poorly written and disappointing.

2 GASCOIGNE, BAMBER. "From the Head." Spectator,
CCIX (July 27, 1962), 115
Plot summaries of Under Plain Cover and The
Blood of the Bamburgs which emphasize that the
plots are frail at best and that whatever mean-
ings exist in them are undiscoverable. The only
reason that the plays were performed at all is
because John Osborne wrote them.

3 _____. Twentieth Century Drama. New York: Hutchin-
son, 1962
Osborne is presented as the progenitor of the
modern renaissance in the English theatre, which
had been in a decline since Shaw. Brief critical comments on Look Back in Anger, The Entertainer, and Luther, which is seen as a vast technical improvement and philosophical progression
from the former naturalistic drama.

59

4 LEWIS, THEOPHILUS. "Theatre." America, CVII (July
      21, 1962), 533-534
         Luther is "superior" to any of Osborne's
      dramas yet performed in the United States. It
      has strong dialogue, but the characterization
      of Luther is too narrow in its historical per-
      spective.

5 "Luther to End Its Run Next Month." London Times
      (February 16, 1962), p.15c
         Luther to be withdrawn on March 29, 1962.

6 "Contempt for Conformists." London Times (July 20,
      1962), p.10e
         The Blood of the Bamburgs is only a "rehash
      of old material" and unsuccessful. Under Plain
      Cover is an innovative study of two lives that
      "connects with the audience like a fist."

7 "High Court of Justice." London Times (November 2,
      1962), p.3d
         Mary Ure's divorce cause against Osborne.

8 "Law Report, Dec. 14." London Times (December 15,
      1962), p.4b
         Mary Ure granted divorce from Osborne.

9 MAGEE, BRYAN. The New Radicalism. London: Secker
      and Warburg, 1962, p.180
         Osborne's The Entertainer is used as an ex-
      ample of an awareness of English conservatism--a
      conservatism that inspires a feeling of pride in
      "doing better than we were" and doing nothing
      more than that.

10 MAROWITZ, CHARLES. "The Ascension of John Osborne."
      Tulane Drama Review, VII (Winter, 1962), 175-179.
      Reprinted in Modern British Dramatists and John

MAROWITZ, CHARLES (cont.)
  Osborne: LOOK BACK IN ANGER, A Casebook.
      Traces Osborne's religious skepticism in his
  portrayals of Jimmy Porter, George Dillon,
  Archie Rice, and Martin Luther. In Luther, Osborne appears to be, like most other modern
  playwrights, under the influence of Brecht. He
  is able to convey in Luther dramatic ideas on a
  poetical level and grasp the twentieth century
  loss of purpose.

11 New York Times (August 9, 1962), p.17:5
      Discusses the filming of Tom Jones.

12 "Filming Tom Jones." New York Times (September 9,
      1962), VI, p.116
        Short statement on the filming of Tom Jones
    and photographs of scenes from the movie.

13 NICOLL, ALLARDYCE. "Somewhat in a New Dimension" in
      Contemporary Theatre. Eds. John Russell Brown
      and Bernard Harris. London: Arnold, 1962, 77-
      95. Reprinted in John Osborne: LOOK BACK IN
      ANGER, A Casebook.
        Discusses Osborne and his contemporaries in
    relation to earlier dramatists of the twentieth
    century. Look Back in Anger's theme was used
    many times in the past, but Osborne's play omits
    all the preliminaries to the action, focuses
    attention on Jimmy Porter and his wife, and ends
    without a conclusion. The World of Paul Slickey
    is used as an example of the modern use of sub-
    jectivity of presentation and the feeling of
    absurdity in the world.

14 ROGERS, DANIEL. "Look Back in Anger--to George
      Orwell." Notes and Queries, IX (1962), 310-311.
        There are two instances in Look Back in Anger

ROGERS, DANIEL (cont.)
   where Jimmy Porter directly quotes George
   Orwell. Orwell's social criticism possesses
   more "fairness" than Osborne's because it gave
   the English ruling class some moral stature.

15 RUPP, GORDON E. "John Osborne and the Historical
    Luther." The Expository Times, LXXIII (Febru-
    ary, 1962), 147-151
        Comments point by point on the chronology of
    Luther compared with other recorded histories
    of Luther's life. Rupp easily shows Osborne's
    dependence on Erik Erikson's Young Man Luther
    and he attempts to put the play in historical
    perspective.

16 STARBUCK, GEORGE. "Damn You, World." Spectator,
    CCIX (October 19, 1962), 584
        The continual invective that comes from Os-
    borne on the degeneracy of England and all of
    Europe suggests that "his immersion in the life
    of Luther could most profitably be followed by
    a long study of William the Silent."

17 TAYLOR, JOHN RUSSELL. The Angry Theater. New York:
    Hill and Wang, 1962, 39-57
        General discussion of Osborne's work from
    Look Back in Anger to Luther in which Brown
    views the first three plays to be far superior
    in dramatic writing, innovation, and empathic
    results to his next three works. Epitaph for
    George Dillon is "the most wholly satisfactory
    of the plays Osborne has worked on," because
    here he does not become so intimately identified
    with the main character. In his later work, the
    resort to factual rather than innovative sub-
    jects may signal the decline of his imaginative
    powers in favor of craftsmanship.

18   ____. Anger and After: A Guide to the New British
        Drama. London: Methuen, 1962, 29-66. Comments
        on Osborne are reprinted in John Osborne: LOOK
        BACK IN ANGER, A Casebook.
            A general review of Osborne's career from his
        early unpublished plays to Plays for England.
        Taylor believes that the progression of Os-
        borne's work is in a process of degeneracy that
        began with The World of Paul Slickey (generally
        agreed to be the worst of Osborne's plays),
        moves to Luther (a non-innovative commercial
        play), and reaches its ultimate low point in
        The Blood of the Bamburgs.

19 TREWIN, J. C. "Hit or Miss." Illustrated London
        News, CCXLI (August 4, 1962), 190
            There is little worthwhile in either of the
        plays. The Blood of the Bamburgs shows Os-
        borne's lack of understanding of the British
        respect for the monarchy. Under Plain Cover
        shows feebleness of dialogue and has no real
        point to make.

20 TYNAN, KENNETH. "Plays for England." London
        Observer (1962). Reprinted in Tynan's Tynan
        Right and Left.*
            Under Plain Cover is the "first overt appear-
        ance" on the English stage of the English sexual
        preoccupation with sado-masochism. The Blood of
        the Bamburgs is "a repetitive joke about royal
        weddings."

21 WESKER, ARNOLD. "Center 42: The Secret Reins."
        Encounter, XXV (March, 1962), 3-6
            Osborne and Look Back in Anger are valid in-
        dicators of the state of contemporary British
        society, which is controlled by the wealthy
        "Lloyd Georges" that forestall change. Wesker

B21   ABOUT JOHN OSBORNE (1962)

WESKER, ARNOLD (cont.)
    calls for the creation of Center 42, an inde-
    pendent cultural arts center, which in part
    would do away with the deficiencies of the Eng-
    lish social system depicted in Osborne's play.

A. Books--1963

None

B. Articles--1963

1 ATKINSON, BROOKS. "Tom Jones Film Version Is a Re-
       minder to Reread Fielding Manuscript." New York
       Times (November 8, 1963), p.28:6
           Praises Osborne and director Tony Richardson
       for capturing the spirit of Fielding's novel.

2 BRUSTEIN, ROBERT. "The Backwards Birds." New Re-
       public, CXLIX (October 19, 1963), 28, 30. Re-
       printed in Brustein's Seasons of Discontent.
           Criticizes Luther for its lack of character
       depth and detail, superficiality, and "lack of
       control."

3 CHAPMAN, JOHN. "Albert Finney Gives Impressive Por-
       trayal in Martin Luther Role." New York Daily
       News (September 26, 1963).* Reprinted in New
       York Theatre Critics' Reviews, XXIV (September
       30, 1963), 277
           Praises all facets of Luther. The play "em-
       bodies dignity, history and drama."

4 "A Layman's Guide to Recent Religious Trends: Os-
       borne's Luther." Christian Century, LXXX (Octo-
       ber 30, 1963), 1351

"A Layman's..." (cont.)
    Osborne's concentration on the physical dif-
ficulties of Luther causes the characterization
to be superficial and the play to be a failure.

5 CLURMAN, HAROLD. "Theatre." Nation, CXCVII (Octo-
       ber 19, 1963), 245-246
       Luther is a very well written play, but it is
    not about the historical Luther. It is Os-
    borne's confessional revelation of the self and
    his problems. The social significance of the
    play is that it expresses the anger of the
    angry young man generation.

6 COLEMAN, ROBERT. "Luther is Recommended." New York
       Mirror (September 26, 1963).* Reprinted in New
       York Theatre Critics' Reviews, XXIV (September
       30, 1963), 276
       Osborne does justice to the character of
    Luther and provides "an excellent vehicle for
    fine actors."

7 CROWTHER, BOSLEY. "Cinematic Tom Jones." New York
       Times (October 13, 1963), II, p.1:8
       Detailed praise of Osborne and Richardson for
    the writing and directing of the movie.

8 DUPREY, RICHARD A. and CHARLES L. PALMS. "Luther."
       Catholic World, CXCVIII (November, 1963), 135-
       136
       Unfavorable of Osborne's handling of reli-
    gious and psychological subjects.

9 DRIVER, TOM F. "Here I Stand (More or Less)."
       Reporter, XXIX (October 24, 1963), 54, 55-56
       Luther evidences Osborne's numerous technical

DRIVER, TOM F. (cont.)
     errors, his inability to deal with reality, and
his capacity for rewriting Jimmy Porter into an
externally different setting while leaving him
the same inside.

10   GASSNER, JOHN. "Broadway in Review." <u>Educational
Theatre Journal</u>, XV (December, 1963), 360-361
     <u>Luther</u> has received undeserved praise because
it relates a sense of importance, but is really
somewhat of a failure.

11   GILL, BRENDAN. "Country Pleasures." <u>New Yorker</u>,
XXXIX (October 12, 1963), 169-170
     Praise for <u>Tom Jones</u>, especially for
Richardson's direction of the movie.

12   GILMAN, RICHARD. "John Osborne's <u>Luther</u>." <u>Common-
weal</u>, LXXIX (October 18, 1963), 103-104
     Feels that Osborne tried for a grand and
epic scope in <u>Luther</u>, a scope which could not
be accomplished by a writing talent such as his.

13   GRIFFIN, EMILIE. "Osborne's <u>Luther</u> Sealed Up."
<u>National Review</u>, XV (November 5, 1963), 446-448,
449
     Praise for Tony Richardson's direction and
Albert Finney's portrayal of Luther, but
Griffin feels that Osborne ultimately fails because he has not taken advantage of the epic
possibilities of Luther's character.

14   GRINDIN, JAMES. <u>Postwar British Fiction</u>. Berkeley:
University of California Press, 1963, 51-64.
Comments on Osborne are reprinted in <u>John Os-
Borne: LOOK BACK IN ANGER, A Casebook</u>.
     <u>Look Back in Anger</u> is a statement on the need
for intimate and particularized communication.

GRINDIN, JAMES (cont.)
It "is less a play about rebellion of the educated young man of the lower classes against
current society than a play about what it means
to give and receive love."

15 HARTUNG, PHILIP T. "Tom Jones." Commonweal, LXXIX,
8 (October 25, 1963), 141
Tom Jones is merely another La Dolce Vita
set in a different time period. Osborne's
script lacks the interest provided in the novel
by Fielding's intrusions.

16 HATCH, ROBERT. "Films." Nation, CXCVII (November
30, 1963), 374
Mixed praise for Tom Jones. No mention of
Osborne.

17 HEWES, HENRY. "Overdoers Undone." Saturday Review,
XLVI (October 12, 1963), 46
Luther is a series of "random thoughts about
a sensitive rebel and the dilemma" which
plagues successful revolutionaries.

18 HUSS, ROY. "John Osborne's Backward Halfway Look."
Modern Drama, VI (May, 1963), 20-25
Psychological study of Jimmy Porter and the
female characters in Look Back in Anger. The
play is a dramatization of pathological behavior,
which primarily takes the forms of the Oedipus
complex, pre-Oedipus, and sado-masochism.

19 KAUFFMANN, STANLEY. "Old Pro and Old Prose." New
Republic, CXLIX (October 19, 1963), 27-28
The movie is an unsuccessful attempt to film
Fielding's Tom Jones because of the "imposing"
and "muddled" attitudes and work of director
Richardson and screenwriter Osborne.

20 KERR, WALTER. "Kerr on Luther at the St. James."
      New York Herald-Tribune (September 26, 1963),
      p.18. Reprinted in New York Theatre Critics'
      Reviews, XXIV (September 30, 1963), 278-279
         Luther presents an analysis of Luther as a
      fractured, physically tortured man who begins a
      world-shaking change without any self-assurance
      of its correctness. The play offers no solu-
      tions, no thorough coherency, but rather a pro-
      vocative exploration of man's action in the
      world.

21   _____. The Theater In Spite of Itself. New York:
      Simon and Schuster, 1963, 129-131
         Reprints Kerr's review of Look Back in Anger
      from the New York Herald-Tribune.

22 KNIGHT, ARTHUR. "Richardson's England." Saturday
      Review, XLVI (October 5, 1963), 52
         Tom Jones is an unsuccessful movie partially
      due to Osborne's script.

23 KNIGHT, G. WILSON. "The Kitchen Sink: On Recent
      Development in Drama." Encounter, XXI (Decem-
      ber, 1963), 48-54
         The productions of the realist-absurdist
      drama in England are psychological releases.
      The realist theatre, led by Osborne, is con-
      cerned with the lower strata of society and ex-
      ists to cure the decaying culture. Analysis of
      Jimmy Porter and Look Back in Anger as leading
      forces of realism.

24 LEWIS, THEOPHILUS. "Reviewer's Notebook." America,
      CVIII (October 26, 1963), 496-497
         Luther misrepresents the historical figure
      as a degenerate man by showing only the super-
      ficial details of his career and giving no

LEWIS, THEOPHILUS (cont.)
>insight into Luther's prime motivation for re-
>volt or the fact that he was aware of the
>economic consequences of his revolt against
>Rome. Those portions of the play which are not
>loose transcriptions of Luther's defiance at
>the Diet of Worms are the redeeming qualities
>of the play. Osborne shows both sides of the
>Protestant-Catholic conflict as corrupt.

25 Life, LV (October 11, 1963), 120-123
>Praise for Tom Jones and the script of the
>"not-so-angry" Osborne.

26 "48 Playwrights in Apartheid Protests." London
>Times (June 26, 1963), p.12d
>Osborne participates in a general withhold-
>ing of plays from the stage by London play-
>wrights.

27 "Luther Impresses New York Critics." London Times
>(September 27, 1963), p.16e
>Quotes from New York theatre critics' re-
>views of Luther.

28 MC CARTEN, JOHN. "Contumacious Theologian." New
>Yorker, IXL (October 5, 1963), 133
>Luther presents an ambivalence of characteri-
>zation, felt here to be a strength. Luther is
>seen as unsure of his actions regarding the
>Peasants Revolt and is realistically portrayed
>as a human being and revolutionary with uncer-
>tain feelings in his approaches to the Papal
>problem.

29 MC CLAIN, JOHN. "Brilliantly Acted Historical
>Drama." New York Journal-American (September
>26, 1963).* Reprinted in New York Theatre

MC CLAIN, JOHN (cont.)
    Critics' Reviews, XXIV (September 30, 1963),
    279
        Luther "will take an early position in the
    hit parade for the new semester."

30 MORGAN, DEREK. "No, But I've Seen the Movie."
        Reporter, XXIX (November 21, 1963), 54
            General praise for Tom Jones, mentioning Os-
        borne's able handling of the script.

31 NADEL, NORMAN. "Osborne's Overpowering Luther."
        New York World-Telegram (September 26, 1963).*
        Reprinted in New York Theatre Critics' Reviews,
        XXIV (September 30, 1963), 277-278
            Praises Luther for presenting a fine dra-
        matic portrayal of Luther's revolutionary char-
        acter and historical discontinuities.

32 "John Osborne Marries." New York Times (May 26,
        1963), p.3:6
            Osborne marries Penelope Gilliatt.

33 "Philadelphia Critics Praise U.S. Premiere of
        Luther." New York Times (September 11, 1963),
        p.46:3
            Summarizes the critical acclaim Luther re-
        ceived in Philadelphia prior to its Broadway
        opening.

34 "T. Jones, Foundling." New York Times (September
        29, 1963), VI, p.104-105
            Brief statement on the filming of Tom Jones
        and photographs of scenes from the movie.

35 "The Two Luthers." Newsweek, LXII (October 7, 1963),
        96
            Praises all facets of Luther and responds to

"The Two Luthers." (cont.)
    other critics who have disliked the play.
    Luther is not a degeneration of a historical
    figure, but a raising of the theatre to the
    heights of epic events.

36 Newsweek, LXII (October 14, 1963), 116-117
        Praises Osborne and director Richardson for
    "conveying the enduring, relevant meaning of
    Fielding's great work."

37 PANTER-DOWNES, MOLLIE. "Letter from London." New
    Yorker, XXXIX (September 7, 1963), 98, 100
        Short note praising Tom Jones.

38 PRIDEAUX, TOM. "A Thirst for Greatness." Life, LV
    (October 11, 1963), 125-126
        Prideaux uses Luther as an opening into com-
    ments on the subject of why there are so few
    modern heroes.

39 PRYCE-JONES, ALAN. "New York Openings: Luther."
    Theatre Arts, XLVIII (December, 1963), 12-13
        The great historical importance and social
    significance of Martin Luther is forsaken in
    Luther in favor of protest cloaked in eloquence.
    The characterization of Luther is as "a monk
    with stomach trouble," rather than as a leader
    of revolt against the established order. Luther
    is more historical pageant than demanding drama.

40 ROGOFF, GORDON. "Portrait of the Artists." New
    Leader, XLVI (October 14, 1963), 27
        Osborne causes the character of Luther to be
    degenerated to half of his real stature. Luther
    appears to be too obsessed with himself and car-
    ing little for his cause.

B41   ABOUT JOHN OSBORNE (1963)

41 SCHLESINGER, ARTHUR M. The Politics of Hope. Bos-
       ton: Houghton Mifflin, 1963, 247-253
          Reprints Schlesinger's review of Look Back
       in Anger from the New Republic.

42 SIMON, JOHN. "Theatre Chronicle." Hudson Review,
       XVI (Winter, 1963-1964), 584-585
          Luther, which is seen as a direct copy of
       Brecht's Galileo, fails because of its hollow
       protagonist and themes that are never developed.
       Osborne is incapable of making characters,
       places, and issues come to life.

43 SMITH, MICHAEL. "Theatre Uptown: Osborne, Anouilh."
       Village Voice (October 2, 1963), p.10
          Luther is a failure in dramatic technique
       and conception. "Osborne seems to have got
       caught between his concern for Martin Luther and
       his concern for today, and while he has impor-
       tant things to say about both, he fails to say
       them in the same breath."

44 TAUBMAN, HOWARD. "Theater: Luther Stars Albert
       Finney." New York Times (September 26, 1963),
       p.41:1. Reprinted in New York Theatre Critics'
       Reviews, XXIV (September 30, 1963), 280
          Although the play might arouse religious
       opinion against it, Osborne has successfully
       written a distinguished drama of epic propor-
       tion. Taubman only disagrees with Osborne's
       use of Luther's bowel problems as the apparent
       cause for his revolutionary actions.

45 "A Good-Intoxicated Man." Time, LXXXII (October 4,
       1963), 63
          Except for Osborne's tendency to dwell on
       Luther's bowel problems, the play is dramatical-
       ly successful and important.

46 Time, LXXXII (October 18, 1963), 117
       Mentions Osborne.

47 WALSH, MOIRA. "Films." America, CIX (November 2,
       1963), 532
       Praises Tom Jones, but only mentions Osborne
       for giving "notable assists" to director
       Richardson.

48 WATTS, RICHARD. "Luther is a Memorable Portrayal."
       New York Post (September 26, 1963).* Reprinted
       in New York Theatre Critics' Reviews, XXIV
       (September 30, 1963), 276
       All aspects of Luther are tremendously suc-
       cessful. "What gives it the chief dramatic ex-
       citement is the sheer theatrical power and skill
       of the writing."

49 WATTS, STEPHEN. "Playwright John Osborne Looks
       Back--And Not in Anger." New York Times (Septem-
       ber 22, 1963), p.1:2
       Osborne discusses Luther and various aspects
       of his career and future outlooks

50 WHITING, JOHN. On Theatre. London: Alan Ross,
       1963
       Reprints Whiting's review of Luther from the
       London Magazine.

51 WORTH, KATHERINE J. "The Angry Young Man: John Os-
       borne" in Experimental Drama. Ed. William A.
       Armstrong. London: G. Bell, 1963, 147-168. Re-
       printed in John Osborne: LOOK BACK IN ANGER, A
       Casebook.
       Osborne's career, themes, and growth are
       analyzed from the first production of Look Back
       in Anger to Luther. In his first play Osborne
       revived the realistic theatre of Shaw and

B51   ABOUT JOHN OSBORNE (1963)

WORTH, KATHERINE J. (cont.)
Galsworthy and showed that realism set in contemporary social situations was still viable on
the English stage. Gradually, his plays became
more innovative and dramatically proficient (except The World of Paul Slickey) until in Luther
Osborne is seen as a much improved playwright
who has considerably widened his dramatic possibilities.

A. Books--1964

None

B. Articles--1964

1 BAXTER, KAY. Speak What We Feel: A Christian Looks
at the Contemporary Theatre. London: SCM Press,
1964
Osborne and other contemporary dramatists ex-
emplify the spiritual depravity of the modern
world and depict the failure of Christianity to
overcome isolation and frustration.

2 BENTLEY, ERIC. The Life of the Drama. New York:
Atheneum, 1964, 287-88
The angry quality of plays such as Look Back
in Anger detract from their dramatic effect, because they are too greatly concerned with the
evocation of pity.

3 BLAU, HERBERT. The Impossible Theatre. New York:
Macmillan, 1964
A discussion of the social theme in Osborne's
Look Back in Anger and The Entertainer, the
author's rebellious nature, and the specific
events behind the polemics of his plays.

4   BRUSTEIN, ROBERT. The Theatre of Revolt. Boston:
       Little, Brown, 1964
          Mentions Osborne in connection with the theme
       of social revolt in modern drama.

5   BRYDEN, RONALD. "Everyosborne." New Statesman,
       LXVIII (September 18, 1964), 410
          This play's success is built upon the fear
       and anxiety aroused in the audience. There is
       a comparison of Osborne's play with Miller's
       Death of a Salesman and a brief comment that
       like Miller's play Inadmissable Evidence is a
       modern Everyman.

6   CARROLL, JOHN T. "Tom Jones." Catholic World,
       CXCIX (April, 1964), 71-72
          Praise for the entire movie and Osborne's
       script, which produces a "compact and vivid"
       portrayal of the lead character.

7   DARLINGTON, W. A. "John Osborne Sets Audience a
       Puzzle." London Daily Telegraph and Morning
       Post (September 10, 1964), p.18
          "Work at it as I would, I could not really
       make out just what Mr. Osborne wanted me to
       find out about his central character, Bill Mait-
       land," in Inadmissable Evidence.

8   DEVLIN, POLLY. "John Osborne." Vogue, CXLIII
       (June, 1964), 98-99, 152, 168
          Biographical article on Osborne's career with
       extensive quotes from an interview. Concen-
       trates on Osborne's personality, angry atti-
       tudes of protest, and patriotism.

9   FRASER, G. S. The Modern Writer and His World.
       Harmondsworth: Penguin, 1964
          The two main influences on Osborne's drama

75

FRASER, G. S. (cont.)
     are Tennessee Williams (on Look Back in Anger)
     and Bertolt Brecht (on The Entertainer and
     Luther). In The Entertainer and Look Back in
     Anger, Osborne uses traditional dialogue and
     stock-characters, but uses the anti-stock re-
     sponse to such subjects as the Royal family, re-
     ligion and patriotism. Jimmy Porter is the
     leader of the angry young man movement because
     of what Adler calls the factor of the masculine
     protest. Porter fails in two of the three main
     areas of human activity, job and community, and
     thus attempts to dominate the third, marriage.
     Brief comments on The World of Paul Slickey and
     Luther.

10 GROSS, JOHN. "1793 and All That." Encounter,
     XXIII (November, 1964), 60
          Inadmissable Evidence is a good play, but as
     with Osborne's other work the writing would have
     to be improved before the protest of the major
     character could be taken as socially indicative.

11 HARDWICK, ELIZABETH. "Theatre." Vogue, CXLIII
     (January 1, 1964), 20
          Luther is "an engrossing, if not profound,
     study of character" and "interesting as a pag-
     eant."

12 HOBSON, HAROLD. "Osborne's New Compassion and Wit."
     Christian Science Monitor (September 14, 1964),
     p.10
          Osborne's study of human failure is not de-
     pressing because of his compassion, wit, and
     theatrical skill.

13 HOLLAND, MARY. "Where's All the Anger Gone?"
        London Observer (September 13, 1964), p.26
        Although Inadmissable Evidence strikes out
    in the normal fashion of Osborne's polemical
    outbursts, it lacks the emotion and anger which
    has been the core of his best work.

14 HUSSEY, CHARLES. "Osborne Looks Forward in Anger."
        New York Times (October 25, 1964), VI, p.71
        General article on Osborne's career which
    promotes the idea that Osborne's anger has not
    diminished with success. A discussion of the
    character of Bill Maitland in Inadmissable Evi-
    dence, Osborne's movie concerns, his fights
    with drama critics, and his participation in
    social protests.

15 KRETZMER, HERBERT. "The Vengeful Cry is Vital."
        London Daily Express (September 10, 1964), p.9
        Osborne's Inadmissable Evidence is "the most
    important new play in years." The comprehension
    of Maitland's failure is accomplished through an
    unmatched dramatic strength.

16 "Return in Embattled First Person." London Times
        (September 10, 1964), p.8d
        Bill Maitland is the successor to Jimmy Port-
    er and Archie Rice and signifies a return in
    Osborne's work to its central theme: the frus-
    tration and feelings of separation in the in-
    dividual. "Mr. Osborne seems alone among cur-
    rent British playwrights in being able to
    create heroes of our own time."

17 "Ban on Osborne Play." London Times (September 17,
        1964), p.10e
        Discussion of the Lord Chamberlain's ban on
    A Patriot for Me, because of its homosexual
    theme. Osborne's reaction to the ban is quoted.

18 "1,314 Arrested in Trafalgar Square Disorders."
    London Times (September 18, 1961), p.10g
         Osborne arrested in anti-nuclear demonstra-
    tion.

19 MACDONALD, DWIGHT. "Films." Esquire, LXI (Febru-
    ary, 1964), 32, 34
         Dislikes Tom Jones and does not mention Os-
    borne.

20 RUTHERFORD, MALCOLM. "Osborne's Language." Specta-
    tor, CCXIII (September 18, 1964), 369-370
         The theme of the fragmentation and disillu-
    sion in life as a middle aged man makes the
    monologue technique necessary in Inadmissable
    Evidence. Maitland's character is analyzed in
    terms of the play's development of this theme.

21 SONTAG, SUSAN. "Going to the Theater." Partisan
    Review, XXX (Winter, 1964), 96-97
         Luther is an instance of a "peculiarly ghoul-
    ish transaction between a bad play and a bad
    audience." The disgusting nature of Osborne's
    concentration on Luther's anality turns a great
    religious leader into the "Great Neurotic."

22 TAYLOR, JOHN RUSSELL. "Inadmissable Evidence."
    Encore, XI, 6 (November-December, 1964), 43-46.
    Reprinted in John Osborne: LOOK BACK IN ANGER,
    A Casebook.
         Taylor is willing to accept the general criti-
    cal opinion that Inadmissable Evidence is Os-
    borne's best play. At last the playwright has
    been able to portray an "elementary truth" about
    his own work: "that his trouble in making char-
    acters connect arises primarily from the fact
    that what really interests him, anguishes him

TAYLOR, JOHN RUSSELL (cont.)
   indeed, is the non-connection of people." The
   failure of communication between characters in
   this play is compared to Fellini's 8 1/2.

23   _____. "British Drama of the Sixties" in On Con-
         temporary Literature. Ed. Richard Kostelanetz.
      New York: Avon, 1964, pp.90-96
         General essay on the British theatre and the
      change it underwent after the production of
      Look Back in Anger. Osborne and the invective
      school are seen only as the quickly dying ini-
      tial phase of this new direction. Even Osborne
      moves out of this style into a more Brechtian
      mode in Luther.

24 TYNAN, KENNETH. Tynan on Theatre. Harmondsworth:
      Penguin, 1964, 130-132, 173-176, 205-207
         Reprints Tynan's review of Look Back in
      Anger, The Entertainer, and Epitaph for George
      Dillon, and his essay "The Angry Young Movement"
      from Holiday.

25 TREWIN, J. C. "Sound and Fury." Illustrated London
      News, CCXLV (September 26, 1964), 480
         Mixed comments on Inadmissable Evidence but
      finally concludes that it will have no lasting
      effect.

26 WARD, A. C. Twentieth Century English Literature.
      London: Methuen, 1964, 11, 138, 140
         Questions the basis for the success of Look
      Back in Anger. If the play had opened original-
      ly in midtown London, it probably would have had
      a much calmer reception.

27 WELLWARTH, GEORGE E. The Theatre of Protest and
        Paradox. New York: New York University Press,
        1964, 221-234. Comments on Osborne are re-
        printed in John Osborne: LOOK BACK IN ANGER, A
        Casebook.
            A discussion of Osborne's plays that particu-
        larly centers on Look Back in Anger and The
        World of Paul Slickey. The former is seen as a
        portrayal of a psychotic marriage situation,
        after the style of Strindberg, and not as the
        herald of a new social revolution. The latter
        is the prototype of the angry young man label
        given to Osborne and is his most direct attack
        upon society. Luther and A Subject of Scandal
        and Concern are more indirect and popularly ac-
        ceptable. Plays for England was Osborne's
        death knell in the theatre; he became a victim
        of his own critical success.

28 WILLIAMS, RAYMOND. "Recent English Drama" in The
        Modern Age. Ed. Boris Ford. Harmondsworth:
        Penguin Brooks, 1964, 487-488, 501-507
            Discusses Osborne, Look Back in Anger, and
        Luther in relation to the contemporary history
        of the English theatre.

29 WORTH, KATHERINE. "Shaw and John Osborne." The
        Shavian, II (1964), 129-135
            Explores various points of comparison be-
        tween Shaw and Osborne, especially their mutual
        affinity for socialism and social protest, the
        symbolic representation of Great Britain, the
        structure of their plays, a shared interest in
        the sexually bizarre, and their "habits of dis-
        tributing dramatic sympathy."

30 YOUNG, B. A. "An Osborne Play Opens in London."
    New York Times (September 10, 1964), p.31:1
         Though it could have used more of Osborne's
    concentration of writing skill, Inadmissable
    Evidence is a successful portrayal of the tor-
    tured Bill Maitland.

31 ZOLOTOW, SAM. "Osborne Discloses London Ban on New
    Play, A Patriot for Me." New York Times (Sep-
    tember 16, 1964), p.36:2
         Quotes Osborne on the Lord Chamberlain's ban
    of A Patriot for Me and discusses the current
    status of Osborne's career.

A. Books--1965

None

B. Articles--1965

1 BRADBROOK, M. C. English Dramatic Form: A History
   of Its Development. New York: Barnes and Noble,
   1965, pp.178, 186-188
        Brief discussion of Osborne's early plays and
   how they reflect a cultural feeling of purpose-
   lessness. "Osborne has great natural theatrical
   ability; he might be called a theatrical jour-
   nalist, for he can quickly turn the mood of the
   day to the forms of the stage, and put it over."

2 BRUSTEIN, ROBERT. "The New English Stage." New
   Statesman, LXX (August 6, 1965), 193-194. Re-
   printed as "The English Stage" in Modern British
   Dramatists.
        Osborne is seen as a natural born dramatist
   that has yet to write a play of lasting value.
   The structure of his plays grows progressively

BRUSTEIN, ROBERT (cont.)
more loose and "have the quality of electrical
particles without a nucleus to hold them in
orbit." The only quality that can account for
his success is the sentimentality that lies be-
neath the veneer of hardness. Brustein criti-
cizes Osborne and other contemporary British
dramatists as being no more than second rate
because their personal affiliations intrude upon
their art.

3   _____. Seasons of Discontent. New York: Simon and
Schuster, 1965, 196-200
Reprints Brustein's "The Backwards Birds"
from New Republic.

4 BRYDEN, RONALD. "Osborne at the Ball." New Statesman, LXX (July 9, 1965), 58
A Patriot for Me is a radical innovation in
the contemporary theatre, which accounts for
much of the criticism it has received. It suf-
fers partially from its length and Osborne's
deficiency in writing forceful and believable
dialogue.

5 CALISHER, HORTENSE. "Will We Get There by Candle-
light?" Reporter, XXXIII (November 4, 1965),
38-40, 42, 44
Lengthy, intelligent analysis of Osborne's
plays the motives felt to be behind them. A
panoramic discussion of Osborne's intellectual
position from 1956 to 1965.

6 CHIARI, J. Landmarks of Modern Drama. London: Jen-
kins, 1965, 109-111
Critical discussions of Look Back in Anger,
The Entertainer, The World of Paul Slickey,

CHIARI, J. (cont.)
   Luther, Plays for England, and Inadmissable Evidence. Included are comments on the general
   critical reactions to the plays and Osborne's
   position among his contemporaries.

7 CLURMAN, HAROLD. "Theatre." Nation, CCI (December
      20, 1965), 508–509. Reprinted in Clurman's The
      Naked Image.
         The play does not create a character out of
      Bill Maitland, but an "image." There is no
      situation portrayed, "only a state of mind."
      Inadmissable Evidence is too strongly pointing
      toward a social cause, an expose of the degener-
      acy of English society.

8 DAVISON, PETER. "Contemporary Drama and Popular
      Dramatic Forms" in Aspects of Drama and the
      Theatre. Sydney: Sydney University Press, 1965,
      227–235
         Osborne has been able to successfully use the
      English music hall for a dual audience response:
      spectator and participant.

9 DUPEE, F. W. "The King of the Cats" and Other Re-
      marks On Writers and Writing. New York: Farrar,
      Straus and Giroux, 1965, 196–200
         Reprints Dupee's essay "England Now—Ariel or
      Caliban" from the Partisan Review.

10 GILMAN, RICHARD. "A Man for These Times." Newsweek,
      LXIX (December 13, 1965), 90. Reprinted in
      Gilman's Common and Uncommon Masks.
         Inadmissable Evidence depicts a new thematic
      focus and a definite sign of maturity in
      Osborne's work. He is no longer concerned with

GILMAN, RICHARD (cont.)
   specific, correctable social ills, but with
   larger, more difficult and abstract corruptions
   in the social establishment.

11 GOTTFRIED, MARTIN. "Inadmissable Evidence."
    Women's Wear Daily (December 1, 1965).* Re-
    printed in Gottfried's Opening Nights: Theatri-
    cal Criticism of the Sixties.
       Mixed review that finds the invective inter-
    esting, but the ideas in Inadmissable Evidence
    simplistic.

12 GROSS, JOHN. "Rebels and Renegades." Encounter,
    XXV (October, 1965), 42
       Judged by the normal naturalistic standards
    of drama, A Patriot for Me is a failure. Gross
    says that he agrees with most critics in this
    assessment. He also attempts to point out a few
    of the play's technical errors.

13 HEWES, HENRY. "Unsentimental Journeys." Saturday
    Review, XLVIII (May 29, 1965), 31
       The character of Bill Maitland is an example
    of society's punishment to an individual who has
    "honesty, love, and good intentions." Maitland's
    generation failed to change the world, but at
    least they have not comfortably adapted to it
    like the younger generation (Maitland's daugh-
    ter). "If Jimmy Porter . . . was Osborne at
    twenty-five, Maitland is Osborne as he sees him-
    self at forty."

14 _____. "England's Summer Season." Saturday Review,
    LII (August 14, 1965), 45
       The protagonist of A Patriot for Me is not
    really the main character, Arthur Redl, "but the

84

_____. (cont.)
     subconscious inner patriotism all of us twist
     into unsatisfactory compromises with society."
     The homosexuality of Redl produces the conflict
     of whether to be a patriot to his country or a
     patriot to his truest personality.

15   _____. "Angry Middle-Aged Man." Saturday Review,
     XLVII (December 18, 1965), 43
          As Bill Maitland tries to remain loyal to his
     own anger and insolence, he alienates everyone
     by his resistance to contemporary life.
     Through Maitland's confrontations and anxieties,
     the complaint of the play is clear. It is the
     castigation of "everything modern in society
     that demeans the individual, wastes his talent,
     and punishes his emotional expression."

16   KERR, WALTER. "Kerr Reviews Inadmissable Evidence."
     New York Herald-Tribune (December 1, 1965),
     p.16. Reprinted in New York Theatre Critics'
     Reviews, XXVI (December 6, 1965), 240
          Inadmissable Evidence is a presentation of
     Bill Maitland as a self-besieged and self-
     judged man whose guilt is indomitable. The
     play is an unforgettable examination in self-
     torture.

17   KRETZMER, HERBERT. "Sprawling Tale With Nothing
     New to Say." London Daily Express (July 1,
     1965), p.4·
          A Patriot for Me is technically deficient and
     thematically redundant.

18   LESLIE, P. "The Angry Young Men Revisited." Kenyon
     Review, XXVII (Spring, 1965), 344-352
          General article on the major figures of the
     angry young man movement and their social

LESLIE, P. (cont.)
environment and how it appears more than a decade after their emergence. The comments on
Osborne stress Look Back in Anger as an early
focal point for the movement. His later works
are seen as moving away from the angry position
to one that is more conventional, but a position that he has yet to master.

19   "Club Production For Osborne Play." London Times
(January 6, 1965), p.5c
Notice that A Patriot for Me will be pre-
sented privately at the Royal Court Theatre be-
cause of censorship restrictions by the Lord
Chamberlain.

20   London Times (January 16, 1965), p.5c
Notice that Inadmissable Evidence will play
in the West End in March, 1965.

21   "Character's Humiliating Ugliness." London Times
(March 18, 1965), p.9c
The breaking of dramatic conventions "hardly
counts" in the assessment of Inadmissable Evidence because of its great "dramatic energy."

22   "Private Staging of Osborne Play." London Times
(May 12, 1965), p.15d
Because of the inability to reconcile the
content of the play with the Lord Chamberlain's
requested changer, A Patriot for Me will be presented at the Royal Court Theatre for members
only. Quotes the English Stage Society Chairman
on why this action was necessary.

23 "John Osborne Play Breaks New Ground." <u>London
    Times</u> (July 1, 1965), p.17c
        <u>A Patriot for Me</u> is a significant advance in
    Osborne's dramatic talent. New attitudes only
    implicit in earlier work emerge in the standard
    Osborne theme of the relationship between the
    world and the separated individual. The writing
    has "a Spacious epic quality," the public and
    private scenes are interwoven, and the play
    possesses "a continuous theatricality."

24 "Marathon Essay on a Nightmare." <u>London Times</u>
    (September 29, 1965), p.14a
        <u>Inadmissable Evidence</u> is "a marathon essay
    in aimless self-laceration."

25 "British Plays Modified for Broadway." <u>London Times</u>
    (December 31, 1965), p.13b
        An account of the state of <u>Inadmissable Evi-
    dence</u> and other British plays after they have
    been produced on the New York stage.

26 MC CARTEN, JOHN. "A Long, Long Wail A-Winding."
    <u>New Yorker</u>, XLI (December 11, 1965), 142-144
        The character of Bill Maitland is too weak
    to fit the angry young man image originally
    created in <u>Look Back in Anger</u>. For this reason,
    <u>Inadmissable Evidence</u> is unsuccessful.

27 MC CARTHY, MARY. "Verdict on Osborne." <u>The Ob-
    server</u> (July 4, 1965), p.17
        <u>A Patriot for Me</u> discussed in the context of
    Osborne's earlier work. The Osborne hero, who
    is always a performer locked into his repetitive
    role, exemplifies the "Osborne nightmare: that
    finally no one will listen." However, Alfred
    Redl fails to compare with Osborne's earlier
    heroes. In light of his previous work, <u>A
    Patriot for Me</u> is a "silly charade."

28 _____. "Patriot or Coward?" The Observer (July 25,
      1965), p.26
           Letter to the editor in response to Kenneth
      Tynan, which answers his criticism of her ar-
      ticle on A Patriot for Me point by point.

29 MC CLAIN, JOHN. "First Night." New York Journal-
      American (December 1, 1965).* Reprinted in New
      York Theatre Critics' Reviews, XXVI (December 6,
      1965), 242. The acting of Nicol Williamson as
      Bill Maitland is superb, but Inadmissable Evi-
      dence itself is confusing and pointless.

30 MAROWITZ, CHARLES, TOM MILNE, AND OWEN HALE, EDS.
      The Encore Reader: A Chronicle of the New Drama.
      London: Methuen, 1965
           Includes Edwin Morgan's "That Uncertain Feel-
      ing," David Watt's "Class Report," Stuart Hall's
      "Beyond Naturalism Pure," and Tom Milne's "The
      Hidden Face of Violence," all of which original-
      ly appeared in Encore.

31 MONTGOMERY, JOHN. The Fifties. London: Allen and
      Unwin, 1965, passim.
           Brief discussion of Osborne as the represen-
      tative angry young man, expressing his disen-
      chantment with and desire to change postwar
      Britain. .The change in British theatre usually
      associated with Osborne's name "was ... in large
      part the creation of John Whiting."

32 MORRIS, IVAN. "In London: A Patriot for Me 'gowned,
      wigged and powdered.'" Vogue, CXLVI (September
      1, 1965), 179
           The play has no thematic point, unless it is
      meant to be a parallel to the Vassall espionage
      case. "It is also far too long and laboured;
      and for a playwright with Osborne's brio the
      writing is strangely muted and humourless."

33 NADEL, NORMAN. "Osborne Play is a Shocker." New
    York World-Telegram (December 1, 1965).* Re-
    printed in New York Theatre Critics' Reviews,
    XXVI (December 1, 1965), 240
        Inadmissable Evidence is a probing, shocking
    analysis of a self-contemptuous man, a "ruth-
    less" and "thorough" characterization that pro-
    duces a successful and overwhelming effect.

34 PANTER-DOWNES, MOLLIE. "Letter from London." New
    Yorker, XLI (April 17, 1965), 176
        Praises Inadmissable Evidence for its dra-
    matic power in the dialogue of Bill Maitland.
    Some remarks on the international audience that
    comes to see "what Osborne and the English are
    up to."

35 _____. "Letter From London." New Yorker, XLI
    (July 31, 1965), 59-60
        Discussion of the homosexual theme in A
    Patriot for Me, some of its flaws in technique,
    and the critical battle over the worth of Os-
    borne's play.

36 RUPP, GORDON. "Luther and Mr. Osborne." Cambridge
    Quarterly, I (Winter, 1965-1966), 28-42
        Erik Erikson's Young Man Luther is the pri-
    mary source for Osborne's Luther. By comparing
    the historical Luther to the play, the psycho-
    logical point for Osborne's work becomes clear.
    Luther presents only the anguish and frustration
    of the character and leaves the more delightful
    aspects of his life out in order to present
    Luther as a figure of rebellion.

37 SEYMOUR, ALAN. "Osborne V.C." London Magazine, V
    (May, 1965), 69-74
        Osborne's drama is a highly personal effort
    without balance or perspective. Look Back in

SEYMOUR, ALAN (cont.)

Anger is "technically cumbersome" and depicts immature attitudes. Epitaph for George Dillon is the best example of Osborne at his worst. The dialogue of Luther lacks the bitterness of his past work and does not rise to the actions of the historical Luther. Plays for England is more effective than any other work and "more exasperatingly over-stated and under written." Inadmissable Evidence is Osborne's discovery that the vicious characters are both the conformist and nonconformist.

38   _____. "Maturing Vision." London Magazine, V (October, 1965), 75-79

There is a progression in Osborne's heroes from Jimmy Porter, who lashed out against society, to Bill Maitland, who partially accepts society, to Colonel Redl, who completely accepts society's evaluation of himself and lives according to its demands only to see that self-betrayal is too strong. When the truth finally is known, Redl "must then flaunt his aberration in society's face until that society has to bring him down." The ambivalence of this response to life is a corollary to Osborne's struggle against bourgeoise society. Osborne is more an objective mature dramatist in A Patriot for Me than in any other.

39   SHEED, WILFRED. "Johnny One-Note." Commonweal, LXXXIII (December 24, 1965), 375. Reprinted in Sheed's The Morning After.

Osborne makes no advance in narrative technique in this play, but he is able to increase

SHEED, WILFRED (cont.)
the depth of his psychological investigation.
Inadmissable Evidence is another and better
variation on Osborne's constant theme of the
"dirty stinking world."

40 SMITH, WARREN SYLVESTER. "New Plays in London."
Christian Century, LXXXII (September 1, 1965),
1066-1067
Both Inadmissable Evidence and A Patriot
for Me deal with "sick" characters. In the
first, Osborne shows the difficulties of an individual in an "open society" and foregoes the
realism of his earlier plays for a more sub-
jective portrayal of his characters. In A
Patriot for Me, "Osborne writes of human dis-
integration and man's resistance to it."

41 SONTAG, SUSAN. "Theatre." Vogue, CXLVI (August 15,
1965), 51-52
Inadmissable Evidence is a failure in terms
of the triviality of its subject and the lack
of a developed dramatic situation. Osborne
is compared unfavorably with Pinter, Wesker, and
Arden.

42 TAUBMAN, HOWARD. "The Theater: Inadmissable
Evidence." New York Times (December 1, 1965),
p.52:1. Reprinted in New York Theatre
Critics' Reviews, XXVI (December 6, 1965),
243
Only a slight touch of optimism saves
Osborne from making Inadmissable Evidence a dire
portrayal of the "dregs and disillusion of
despair."

43 "Hell's Isolation Ward." Time, LXXXVI (December 10,
    1965), 76
        Inadmissable Evidence is an incisive analysis
    of man's feelings of isolation and guilt. Os-
    borne is searching throughout all of his plays
    for an organic re-harmonization of man with the
    world. His anger results from his special type
    of caring.

44 TREWIN, J. C. Drama in Britain 1951-1964. London:
    Longmans, Green, 1965.
        General name and date history of British
    drama in which Osborne is frequently mentioned.

45 TYNAN, KENNETH. "Missing Osborne's Point."
    London Observer (July 18, 1965), p.26
        Letter to the editor in response to Mary
    McCarthy's review of A Patriot for Me. The play
    is strongest where McCarthy feels that it is
    weakest. "I suspect that Miss McCarthy is
    really chastising Osborne for eluding her
    pigeon-hole, for extending his range to places
    and periods beyond her foretelling."

46 WATT, DOUGLAS. "Osborne's Inadmissable Evidence
    Story of a Solicitor in Collapse." New York
    Daily News (December 1, 1965).* Reprinted in
    New York Theatre Critics' Reviews, XXVI (Decem-
    ber 6, 1965), 242
        The play fails because the tragedy it con-
    cerns is portrayed without feeling.

47 WATTS, RICHARD. "The Downfall of a Man of Law."
    New York Post (December 1, 1965).* Reprinted in
    New York Theatre Critics' Reviews, XXVI, 16
    (December 6, 1965), 241
        Inadmissable Evidence is unsatisfying because
    of its complete concentration on the character
    of Bill Maitland.

JOHN OSBORNE: A REFERENCE GUIDE

A. Books--1966

1   John Osborne: A Symposium. London: Royal Court
        Theatre, 1966.
            On the tenth anniversary of the opening per-
        formance of Look Back in Anger at the Royal
        Court Theatre, a number of individuals--such as
        John Arden, Alan Sillitoe, and Angus Wilson--
        give their appraisal of Osborne's significance
        in the British theatre.

B. Articles--1966

1   ANDERSON, LINDSAY. "A Bond Honoured." London Times
        (June 24, 1966), p.13d
            Letter to the editor giving six points on why
        John Osborne should be supported against the
        critics. The critics are little better than
        philistines.

2   ARDEN, JOHN. "A Bond Honoured." London Times
        (June 11, 1966), p.11c
            Letter to the editor condemning the critics
        of A Bond Honoured for not fully appraising the
        play because of their inadequate research into
        the play's history. Supports Osborne's posi-
        tion.

3   BARKER, CLIVE. "Look Back in Anger--The Turning
        Point." Zeitschrift fur Anglistik und Amerika-
        nistik, XIV (1966), 367-371
            Look Back in Anger was a necessary transi-
        tional play between the old and new styles of
        the British theatre, which allowed a number of
        young playwrights (i.e., Delaney and Behan) to
        break with the old style typified by Eliot and
        Whiting and eventually go beyond Osborne.

4   BATTESTIN, M. C. "Osborne's Tom Jones: Adapting a
        Classic." Virginia Quarterly, XLII (1966), 378–
        393. Reprinted in Man and the Movies.
            Differences between the movie and the novel
        Tom Jones must necessarily exist: the former is
        directed out of a world view of disorder, while
        the latter exemplifies the orderly nature of
        the world. What was achieved in the movie
        adaptation was the capturing of the spirit of
        the novel. The essential point of judgment is
        "to evaluate the skill of its makers in striking
        analogous rhetorical techniques." In this re-
        spect, Tom Jones is "one of the most successful
        adaptations in the brief history of film."

5   BETJEMAN, JOHN. "A Bond Honoured." London Times
        (June 18, 1966), p.11d
            Letter to the editor. The play was "tremen-
        dous" and "profound." The critics who had to
        write hurried reviews disliked the play, but
        those who had more time to think praised it.

6   BRIEN, ALAN. "Theatre." Vogue, CXLVIII (September
        1, 1966), 206
            A Bond Honoured is "a serious, ambitious, and
        valuable play, too rich and meaty for one sit-
        ting, which matures in the memory."

7   BRUSTEIN, ROBERT. "Osborne's Elegiac Monody." New
        Republic, CLIV (January 1, 1966), 34–35. Re-
        printed in The Third Theatre.
            Inadmissable Evidence possesses a "blistering
        rhetoric" and "a fascinating self-lacerating
        protagonist." The play also gives too much time
        to Osborne's "editorials" of invective, and the
        characters are just as one-dimensional as those
        in his earlier work.

8 CARTER, A. V. "John Osborne: A Re-Appraisal." Re-
    vue Belge de Philologie et d'Histoire, XLIV
    (1966), 971-976
        Osborne's plays are presentation of charac-
    ters who are unable to communicate, find them-
    selves uncaring about other problems than their
    isolation from the rest of mankind, and arouse
    sympathy in audiences for their deplorable
    situation. Osborne attempts to portray our
    problems, not to solve them, and to go beyond
    the modern feeling of futility. "Osborne can
    be called a realist, if realism is taken to
    mean the psychological exploration of contempo-
    rary reality."

9 CLINTON, FARLEY. "Look Back With Nausea." National
    Review, XVIII (April 5, 1966), 325-326
        "I must warn you that the play [Inadmissable
    Evidence] is lousy, and that you will only be
    puzzled, annoyed, embarrassed and disgusted if
    you waste time and money on it."

10 CLURMAN, HAROLD. The Naked Image. New York: Mac-
    millan, 1966, 101-104
        Reprints Clurman's review of Inadmissable
    Evidence from Nation.

11 COHEN, MARSHALL. "Theater 66." Partisan Review,
    XXXIII, 2 (Spring, 1966)
        Inadmissable Evidence marks a "recovery" from
    Luther. Although Osborne is a fine journalist
    in his expression of social discontent, the
    technical lapses in all of his plays ultimately
    prove the works unsatisfactory.

12 COLEMAN, ARTHUR AND GARY R. TYLER. Drama Criticism.
    Denver: Swallow Press, 1966, 169-171
        Selected and unannotated checklist of criti-
    cism on individual Osborne plays.

13 CORRIGAN, ROBERT W. "Theatre." Vogue, CXLVII (Jan-
    uary 15, 1966), 34
         While the subject matter of Inadmissable Evi-
    dence could be dull, the actors provide the
    brilliance through their reactions as well as
    their delivery.

14 DOWNER, ALAN S. "Total Theatre and Partial Drama:
    Notes on the New York Theatre, 1965-1966." The
    Quarterly Journal of Speech, LII (October,
    1966), 225-236
         Inadmissable Evidence is an "insistent reve-
    lation" of the uglier side of contemporary life.
    The play is a compelling drama, which demon-
    strates Osborne's ability to "act creatively"
    within traditional theatrical conventions. The
    play is compared to Miller's Death of a Salesman.

15 DUKORE, BERNARD. "Portrait of a Would-Be Artist."
    Western Speech, XXX (Spring, 1966), 68-81
         Extensive criticism of the character of
    George Dillon as a non-artist in Epitaph for
    George Dillon. Dillon is a man who succumbs to
    the middle class temptations and is destroyed
    by them. The role of the character, his rele-
    vance to theme, and how his development is ac-
    complished by Osborne and Creighton are dis-
    cussed.

16 ELSOM, JOHN. "A Bond With Nahum Tate." London
    Magazine, VI, 8 (November, 1966), 73-76
         Criticizes Osborne's adaptation of La fianza
    satisfecha in A Bond Honoured for its lack of
    sympathy and verity.

17 ESSLIN, MARTIN. "Where Angry Young Men Led." New
    York Times (May 8, 1966), II, p.4:5
         Written on the tenth anniversary of the
    first production of Look Back in Anger.

ESSLIN, MARTIN (cont.)
Osborne's play was the first successful break-
through into modern British drama and resulted
from his willingness to break "the shackles of
the convention of language which is the true
measure of the change in the cultural clime
wrought by the Royal Court during these last
ten years."

18   _____. "Brecht and the English Stage." Tulane
Drama Review, XI (Winter, 1966), 63-70
Mentions Brecht's influence on Osborne.

19   GASSNER, JOHN. "Broadway Review." Educational
Theatre Journal, XVIII (March, 1966), 59-60
Inadmissable Evidence lacks the depth of
character study found in Epitaph for George
Dillon. The character of Bill Maitland could
have been more appropriately handled in a one
act play. "Much as one might be grateful for
seeing another play by this gifted writer, I
can only wonder whether, so to speak, Osborne's
ingenious game is worth the candle."

20   KUTHKE, KARL S. Modern Tragicomedy. New York:
Random House, 1966, 77, 143
Brief comments on The Entertainer as a
tragicomedy.

21   HARTLEY, WALTER. "Useful Criticism." London Times
(June 15, 1966), p.13d
Letter to the editor supporting Osborne.
Contrary to Osborne's opinion the critics are
useful, because when they say a play is bad, it
is assuredly good; when they say it is good, it
never is.

B22   ABOUT JOHN OSBORNE (1966)

22 HEWES, HENRY. "Unsubmissive Performance." Satur-
       day Review, XLIX (January 8, 1966), 96
          A discussion of the themes of separation in
       the actor's response to the part of Bill Mait-
       land in Inadmissable Evidence. Maitland is put
       through a series of confrontations with people
       he considers to be inadmissable in order to re-
       veal the protagonist to himself.

23 HIGGINS, JOHN. "Mother's Days." Spectator, CCXVI
       (June 17, 1966) 760-761
          In the controversy over A Bond Honoured, the
       truth obviously lies somewhere between the two
       extremes. The play itself is a mixture of
       dazzling sights and rather dull sounds.

24 JONES, D. A. N. "Hot Thing." New Statesman, LXXI
       (June 17, 1966), 902
          Osborne's A Bond Honoured, a reworking of
       Lope de Vega's drama, is a caustic remark on the
       decadence of English society.

25 KERSHAW, JOHN. The Present Stage. London: Fontana,
       1966, pp.21-41
          The power of Look Back in Anger derives from
       its concern with people and their social circum-
       stances and the audiences' emotional involve-
       ment, rather than a concern with events or ex-
       ternal situations. The play's language is ad-
       mirably suited to the personality and back-
       ground of the characters, and for the first time
       British drama is able to break out of its usual
       middle class speech conventions. "Look Back in
       Anger is an important play because it brings
       contemporary reality to the stage; a sense of
       the true underlying mood of the 'fifties.'"

26 KITCHIN, LAURENCE. Drama in the Sixties. London:
        Faber and Faber, 1966, pp.185-191
            "Redbrick Luther" is a discussion of Luther
        as the somewhat dubious progression of Osborne
        into a recognized international dramatist. Os-
        borne is in the mainstream of contemporary the-
        atrical achievements.

27 KOTLOWITZ, ROBERT. "Multiple Temptations."
        Harper's, CCXXXII (April, 1966), 125
            Praises Nicol Williamson's performance as
        Bill Maitland, but feels that "the play itself
        was less satisfactory, attempting a few too
        many theatrical tricks that made us all too
        aware of the author's techniques."

28 KRETZMER, HERBERT. "Osborne Staggers--Then Limps."
        London Daily Express (June 7, 1966), p.6
            A Bond Honoured is the most extreme example
        of vituperation in contemporary drama. Osborne
        seems to say that the man who is honest with
        himself cannot help but experience a thorough-
        going rejection of everything in his life.

29 LELYVELD, JOSEPH. "Osborne Assails Critics." New
        York Times (June 9, 1966), p.53:1
            Discussion of Osborne's letter to the London
        theatre critics claiming that they are intellec-
        tually "puny." Quotes from Osborne's letter and
        the critics' reactions.

30 LEWIS, THEOPHILUS. "Theatre." America, CXIV, 2
        (January 8, 1966), 54
            "There is not protest" in this play, "and in-
        cidentally no drama--only the Hogarthian por-
        traiture of a rake near the end of the line."

31 "Revival Arrives Too Late After 350 Years." London
        Times (June 7, 1966), p.14a
            Scathing review of A Bond Honoured which is
        nothing more than "the Osborne ego raised to a
        pitch of delirious omnipotence." The "self-
        indulgence" on Osborne's part and the outworn
        sadism in the play make it a total failure.

32 "Happy Families in the Theatre." London Times
        (June 8, 1966), p.13e
            The general consensus of critical opinion on
        A Bond Honoured is that the play is "boring,"
        "bunkum," and "decidedly uncosy."

33 "Mr. Osborne Looks On In Anger." London Times
        (June 9, 1966), p.14d
            Comments on Osborne's "puny critics" state-
        ment.

34 "Mr. Osborne Claims Support." London Times (June
        10, 1966), p.12e
            In the running battle over A Bond Honoured
        between Osborne and the critics, Osborne now
        claims the support of such people as Lindsay
        Anderson, Arnold Wesker, and John Dexter in his
        assertion that critics are "frivolous" and "ir-
        responsible" when faced with a serious play.

35 MACFADYEN, JOANA. "A Bond Honoured." London Times
        (June 10, 1966), p.13d
            Letter to the editor supporting Osborne in
        his fight with the critics. Mrs. MacFadyen
        writes that she is a frequent playgoer, enjoyed
        Osborne's play, and has never met the playwright.

36 New York Times (April 6, 1966), p.36:4
        The New York production of Inadmissable Evi-
    dence will be withdrawn on April 23, 1966.

37 "Notes and Comment." New Yorker, XLII (October 8,
    1966), 47-48
        Remarks on the "blessed alchemy of word of
    mouth," a statement used by Osborne to account
    for his popularity.

38 PLAYFAIR, GILES. "Phoney War." Spectator, CCXVI
    (June 17, 1966), 754
        Discussion of Osborne's battle with the
    critics. The theatre "cannot live, or at least
    progress, without critics. If it will not ex-
    plore ways of helping them it had better support
    them in silence."

39 PRIDEAUX, TOM. "Narcissus Spitting at His Own
    Image." Life, LX (January 14, 1966), 17
        Praises Inadmissable Evidence and discusses
    some of the difficulties surrounding the Broad-
    way production.

40 RICHARDSON, JACK. "The Best of Broadway." Commen-
    tary, XLI (March, 1966), 75
        Inadmissable Evidence is "a brilliant collec-
    tion of notes for a play."

41 ROBERTS, KEITH. "Mr. Osborne and the Critics."
    London Times (June 13, 1966), p.11c
        Letter to the editor answering Osborne's ob-
    jections to the critical response toward A Bond
    Honoured. Roberts generally feels that Osborne
    is incapable of accepting criticism of any sort.

42 ROGOFF, GORDON. "Richard's Himself Again: Journey
        to an Actor's Theatre." Tulane Drama Review,
        XI (Winter, 1966), 29-40
            Osborne's drama had the appearance of revolu-
        tionary innovation when it first appeared, but
        in retrospect and with the knowledge of his
        later work it now appears that Osborne is "more
        a figure from the past than from the present.
        . . . True, he seemed to start a movement, but
        it was left for others to set that movement
        into searching, less nostalgic, motion."

43 SIMON, JOHN. "Theatre Chronicle." Hudson Review,
        XIX (Spring, 1966), 112-113
            The play declines after the first act into a
        stream of invective. Its two problems are a
        lack of form and "wholly convincing motivation."
        Inadmissable Evidence is a "postlapsarian freak
        show," whose virtues will allow it to survive.

44 TAYLOR, JOHN RUSSELL. "Ten Years of the English
        Stage Company." Tulane Drama Review, XI (Win-
        ter, 1966), 120-131
            A general discussion of the English Stage
        Company's first decade with comments on Os-
        borne's Look Back in Anger, The Entertainer,
        Luther, Inadmissable Evidence, and A Patriot
        for Me.

45 TRILLING, OSSIA. "A Bond Honoured." London Times
        (June 20, 1966), p.11d
            The management of a theatre has the responsi-
        bility to see that the critics are informed
        about the plays it presents.

46 TREWIN, J. C. "Grooves of Change." Illustrated
        London News, CCXLVIII (June 18, 1966), 33
            A Bond Honoured is acceptable, but the real
        question is, why was it produced?

47 TRUSSLER, SIMON. "His Very Own Golden City: Inter-
        view." Tulane Drama Review, XI (Winter, 1966),
        192-202
            In this interview, Arnold Wesker comments on
        Osborne's effect on himself and the British
        theatre.

48 TURNSTILE, M. "Puny Critics." New Statesman,
        LXXII (June 17, 1966), 874
            A discussion of the critics' reactions to A
        Bond Honoured and Osborne's response to the
        play's unfavorable reviews.

49 WARDLE, IRVING. "Osborne and the Critics." New
        Society (June 16, 1966), pp. 22-23
            A response to Osborne's reaction to the over-
        night criticism of A Bond Honoured. Wardle
        criticizes Osborne's unwillingness to face his
        critics in a direct confrontation over their
        differences, but praises him as the best current
        dramatist and notes the essential quality of his
        "monodramas": the interaction of the main char-
        acter with the audience.

50 WEIGHTMAN. J. "Heroes of Our Time." Encounter,
        XXVII (August, 1966), 45-47
            Compares A Bond Honoured with Wesker"s Their
        Very Own Golden City and finds them both to be
        failures. Osborne's play is another return of
        Jimmy Porter, this time in the guise of a Span-
        ish aristocrat, and the usual diatribe against
        society.

51 WILSON, E. M. "A Bond Honoured." London Times
        (June 14, 1966), p.13d
            Letter to the editor giving the facts of the
        historical background of Lope de Vega's La
        fianza satisfecha.

AO   ABOUT JOHN OSBORNE (1967)

A. Books--1967

None

B. Articles--1967

1 ADELMAN, IRVING AND RITA DWORKIN. Modern Drama: A
       Checklist of Critical Literature on Twentieth
       Century Plays. Metuchen, New Jersey: Scarecrow
       Press, 1967, pp.236-238
           Includes a selective and unannotated check-
       list of general criticism and criticism of in-
       dividual Osborne plays (The Entertainer, Look
       Back in Anger, Luther, and The World of Paul
       Slickey).

2 BAXTER, K. M. Contemporary Theatre and the Chris-
       tian Faith. New York: Abingdon, 1967, pp.79-88
           Discussion of the Christian themes in Look
       Back in Anger, The Entertainer, and Luther. The
       moralizing conclusions on each of the plays are
       unique interpretations, but are rather minor
       themes in the scope of each play.

3 CAGERNE, WALTER, Ed. The Playwrights Speak. New
       York: Walter Wager, 1967, pp.127-138
           This is an interview that took place January
       21, 1962, on the BBC's "Face to Face." It is
       preceded by a brief discussion of Osborne's
       career up to that time.

4 FREEDMAN, MORRIS. The Moral Impulse. Carbondale:
       University of Southern Illinois Press, 1967,
       pp.116-117
           Comparison of Jimmy Porter and Stanley Kowal-
       ski from A Streetcar Named Desire. These two
       are seen as different examples of alienation
       from the social establishment. Porter will have

FREEDMAN, MORRIS (cont.)
    nothing to do with the world that is organized
    around government and politics and makes only
    gestures to accommodate society. Kowalski ac-
    cepts society as it is, "defies it, but accepts
    its simple-minded values."

5 GERSH, GABRIEL. "The Theatre of John Osborne."
       Modern Drama, X (September, 1967), 137-143
       General discussion of Osborne's plays to
    1968. The article centers on the plays' major
    themes viewed through the major characters and
    their relationship to Osborne's need for an
    enemy. The change in focus of his work from
    personal enemy to public enemy back to personal
    enemy is generated from his theatrical and
    financial success as a playwright.

6 LUMLEY, F. New Trends in Twentieth Century Drama.
       London: Barrie and Rockliff, 1967, pp.221-232
       General study of Osborne's first decade of
    work, from Look Back in Anger to A Bond
    Honoured. The change in Osborne's attitude
    from the angry young man to a mature dramatist
    is easily seen, but his invective may have sui-
    cidal effects. High praise for the general
    scope of his work.

7 "Mr. John Osborne Is Sued for Film Injunction."
       London Times (February 22, 1967), p.7a
       Osborne is sued over copyright infringement
    for his film script "The Charge of the Light
    Brigade."

8 "When an Author Has Freedom To Quote." London Times
       (February 23, 1967), p.9d
       Discussion of the general circumstances of
    copyright infringement with specific reference
    to Osborne and his script for "The Charge of the
    Light Brigade."

B9   ABOUT JOHN OSBORNE (1967)

9   "Script Not Based on Books, Says Mr. Osborne."
        London Times (February 24, 1967), p.20e
            Osborne's defense in the case over "The
        Charge of the Light Brigade."

10 "Concession on Quotations." London Times (February
        25, 1967), p.17f
            Deals with the "Charge of the Light Brigade"
        case.

11 "Crimean War Film Injunction Against Mr. Osborne."
        London Times (March 21, 1967), p.20g
            Injunction against Osborne for copyright in-
        fringement in his script for "The Charge of the
        Light Brigade."

12 "Divorce Suit Against Osborne." London Times
        (August 19, 1967), p.2c
            Penelope Gilliatt files for a divorce from
        Osborne.

13 "Decree for Wife of John Osborne." London Times
        (December 5, 1967), p.2c
            Penelope Gilliatt granted divorce from Os-
        borne.

14 MAROWITZ, CHARLES AND SIMON TRUSSLER. Theater at
        Work: Playwrights and Productions in the Modern
        British Theater. New York: Hill and Wang, 1967,
        46-47, 83-84
            Reprints Simon Trussler's interview with
        Arnold Wesker "His Very Own Golden City" from
        the Tulane Drama Review. In Irving Wardle's in-
        troduction, Osborne is discussed in relation to
        the changing focus of British drama since Look
        Back in Anger.

15 "John Osborne is Divorced." New York Times (Decem-
      ber 5, 1967), p.59:2
        Osborne is divorced by Penelope Gilliatt.

16 POPKIN, HENRY. "Brechtian Europe." Drama Review
      XII (Fall, 1967), 156-157
        Discusses Luther as a Brechtian play.

17 SPANOS, WILLIAM V. The Christian Tradition in
      Modern British Verse Drama. New Brunswick, New
      Jersey: Rutgers University Press, 1967, pp.336-
      337
        Mentions Look Back in Anger.

18 TAYLOR, JOHN RUSSELL. The Rise and Fall of the Well-
      Made Play. New York: Hill and Wang, 1967, 162
        Mentions Osborne in general comments on the
      contemporary theatre.

19 "A Weakness for Causes." Time, XC (September 8,
      1967), 45
        Mentions Osborne's contribution to the 1967
      Encounter survey on the social opinions of con-
      temporary writers.

20 TYNAN, KENNETH. Tynan Right and Left. New York:
      Atheneum, 1967, 77-78, 83-84, 109-110, 179-181
        Reprints Tynan's review of Plays for England
      from the London Observer.

A. Books--1968

1 HAYMAN, RONALD. John Osborne. New York: Ungar,
      1968. [Revised 1972]
        General study of Osborne's work with chapter
      length examination of the individual plays from
      Look Back in Anger to West of Suez. Hayman
      stresses the concern for the individual hero in

HAYMAN, RONALD (cont.)
Osborne's work, frequently showing how this concern works against a fullness of dramatic ex-
pression and locks Osborne into a repeated pat-
tern. The book includes a list of stage productions and cast lists for all of the London
and New York premieres.

2   TAYLOR, JOHN RUSSELL, Ed. John Osborne: LOOK BACK
IN ANGER, A Casebook. London: Macmillan, 1968
This casebook includes twenty first per-
formance (London) reviews of Look Back in Anger,
five prose works by Osborne ("The Writer in His
Age," "The Epistle to the Philistines," "That
Awful Museum," "A Letter to my Fellow Country-
men," and "On Critics and Critics and Criti-
cism"), eight critical studies (John Russell
Taylor's "John Osborne," Katherine Worth's "The
Angry Young Man," George E. Wellwarth's "John
Osborne: 'Angry Young Man'?" Geoffrey Carnall's
"Saints and Human Beings: Orwell, Osborne and
Ghandi," Edwin Morgan's "That Uncertain Feel-
ing," John Mander's "The Writer and Commitment,"
Mary McCarthy's "A New Word," Charles Marowitz's
"The Ascension of John Osborne"), three foreign
reviews by Harold Clurman, John Gassner, and Guy
Dumur; and nine "points of view" on the play
(Allardyce Nicoll's "Somewhat in a New Dimen-
sion," from Laurence Kitchin's Mid-Century
Drama, from James Grindin's Postwar British Fic-
tion, "An Osborne Symposium from the National
Theatre Program," Lindsay Anderson's "Stand Up,
Stand Up," Stuart Hall's "Something to Live
For," and an extract by Tom Milne from Encore).
Taylor's introduction provides an overview of
the play and its contemporary social milieu and
a discussion of some of the criticism Look Back
in Anger has received. In the "General Editor's

TAYLOR, JOHN RUSSELL, Ed. (cont.)
Comments," A. E. Dyson gives a critical analy-
sis and something of a personal response to
Osborne's play.

B. Articles--1968

1 BARNES, CLIVE. "Theater: New Osborne and Bowen
      Plays in London." New York Times (July 5, 1968),
      p.20:1
          Osborne's anger is generally without direc-
      tion. Time Present lacks innovation and is "a
      feeble, passionless play."

2 _____. "The Theater: John Osborne's The Hotel in
      Amsterdam." New York Times (August 17, 1968),
      p.17:1
          The play succeeds primarily because of Paul
      Scofield's acting. Osborne's drama is only
      about his own life, whatever changes occur,
      occur in both.

3 BATTESTIN, M. C. "Osborne's Tom Jones: Adapting a
      Classic" in Man and the Movies. Ed. W. R. Rob-
      inson. Baton Rouge: Louisiana State University
      Press, 1968, pp.31-45
          Reprints Battestin's article from the Vir-
      ginia Quarterly Review.

4 BOWEN, JOHN. "Theatre: Remembrance of Things Past."
      London Magazine, VIII (August, 1968), 89-90
          Time Present is an embarrassing failure.

5 _____. "Theatre: The Hotel in Amsterdam." London
      Magazine, VIII (September, 1968), 102-106
          This is not a "story" play, but an investi-
      gation into a facet of human behavior. Traces
      Osborne's past work and critical reception.

6 BROWN, JOHN RUSSELL, Ed. Modern British Dramatists.
   Englewood Cliffs: Prentice-Hall, 1968
        In his introduction, Brown discusses the
   general scope of modern British drama and the
   major playwrights. He comments briefly on Look
   Back in Anger, Luther, Inadmissable Evidence, A
   Bond Honoured, A Patriot for Me, and Plays for
   England. Included in this collection of ar-
   ticles are Raymond Williams' "New English Drama"
   A. E. Dyson's "Look Back in Anger," Charles
   Marowitz's "The Ascension of John Osborne," and
   Robert Brustein's "The English Stage."

7 BRYDEN, RONALD. "Daughter in Revolt." London Observer (May 26, 1968), p.30
        Time Present's beginning is quite dull and
   something like Noel Coward, but as it goes on
   Osborne's invective begins to flow more steadily
   and the play is partially redeemed. Osborne has
   created a strong and well-rounded central character in his "most mature, least self-indulgent
   play."

8 _____. "Studies in Survival." London Observer
   (July 7, 1968), p.24
        The Hotel in Amsterdam is a study in social
   corruption. Taken with Time Present and Inadmissable Evidence, Osborne has written some of
   the most important dramatic works of the 1960's.
   It is only a shame that these plays are frag-
   mented into three separate pieces.

9 ESSLIN, MARTIN. "Now, Osborne's Angry Young Woman."
   New York Times (June 2, 1968), II, p.3:6
        The conventional setting of Time Present, the
   dated plot line, and the distracting strident
   dialogue block an interesting idea (the latent
   homosexual relationship) from succeeding.

110

10 FRENCH, PHILIP. "The View Lengthwise." New States-
      man, LXXVI (July 12, 1968), 59-60
          Time Present and The Hotel in Amsterdam are
      both too long, lack action, and are too loosely
      constructed. Osborne is at a time when he's
      working too close to his material." If these
      plays had been tightened and presented together,
      the effect would have been tremendous.

11 GASSNER, JOHN. Dramatic Soundings. New York:
      Crown, 1968, pp.612-614
          Generally despairing comments on Look Back in
      Anger, Inadmissable Evidence, and Plays for Eng-
      land.

12 HEILMAN, ROBERT BECHTOLD. Tragedy and Melodrama:
      Versions of Experience. Seattle: University of
      Washington Press, 1968
          Brief comments on Look Back in Anger and In-
      admissable Evidence.

13 HOBSON, HAROLD. "Osborne's Latest." Christian
      Science Monitor (August 7, 1968), p.12
          The Hotel in Amsterdam, "a play of substance
      and thought," is one of the greatest English
      dramatic successes in years.

14 _____. "Anger as of Now." Christian Science Moni-
      tor (November 6, 1968), p.6
          The fame of Look Back in Anger in 1956 was
      almost political, but in its 1968 revival the
      play is also seen to be "a moving psychological
      and domestic tragedy."

15 KRETZMER, HERBERT. "A New Osborne Kicks Itself to
      Death." London Daily Express (May 24, 1968),
      p.8
          Time Present is evidence that Osborne has not

111

KRETZMER, HERBERT (cont.)
   lost his power for invective, but it also gives
   no evidence that he has improved as a playwright.

16 LAHR, JOHN. "Poor Johnny One-Note." Evergreen Re-
       view, XII (December, 1968), 61-63, 93-95
          Since the time of Look Back in Anger, Os-
       borne has grown progressively less angry and
       dramatically "flabby." As a dramatist, he and
       his message have outlived their time of inten-
       sity and meaning. "In the name of hardness, he
       settles for facility; under the guise of
       honesty, he indulges boredom until it becomes
       amateurish."

17 LAWSON, NIGEL. "Catcalls." Spectator, CCXXI (July
       19, 1968), 97-98
          Time Present lacks subtlety and is melodra-
       matic. It fails primarily because Osborne has
       not yet fully thought out his new conservative
       political position.

18 LEWIS, ANTHONY. "London Revives Look Back in Anger,
       Still a Hit." New York Times (November 1, 1968),
       p.38:1
          The revival of Look Back in Anger reveals
       that the play was not really concerned with
       social protests, but with more universal ele-
       ments of human character. Quotes a number of
       critics on their reactions to seeing the play
       again.

19 "Osborne's Random Sortie." London Times (January
       23, 1968), p.81
          Comments on Osborne's current work.

20 "Judgement Reserved in Osborne Case." London Times
       (March 1, 1967), p.7e
          Postponement of judgement in Osborne's copy-
       right infringement case.

21 "Osborne Play With Schofield." London Times (March
       7, 1968), p.7d
          The pre-production notice for The Hotel in
       Amsterdam.

22 "Osborne's New Plays." London Times (May 14, 1968),
       p.15f
          Production notices for Time Present and The
       Hotel in Amsterdam.

23 "John Osborne Weds Actress." New York Times (April
       20, 1968), p.25:6
          Osborne marries Jill Bennett.

24 "Osborne, Recanting, Is Happy to be Alive and Well
       in London." New York Times (September 4, 1968),
       p.40:3
          Quotes Osborne's letter to the London Times
       (September 3, 1968) in which he apologizes for
       his "damn you England" comment made "several
       years ago."

25 NOVICK, JULIUS. Beyond Broadway. New York: Hill
       and Wang, 1968, 150-151
          Mentions Osborne and the off-off-Broadway
       productions of his plays.

26 PALMER, HELEN H. AND ANNE JANE DYSON. European
       Drama Criticism. Hamdon, Connecticut: Shoe
       String Press, 1968, pp.305-310
          A selected and unannotated checklist of
       criticism on Osborne for the period 1957 to
       1965.

ABOUT JOHN OSBORNE (1968)

27 PRIDEAUX, TOM. "Johnny's Dying One-Note." Life,
       LXV (August 2, 1968), 10
           Osborne's themes and protests have become
       static in his latest plays.

28 ROGERS, DANIEL. "'Not for Insolence, But Serious-
       ly': John Osborne's Adaptation of La fianza
       satisfecha." Durham University Journal, (1968),
       pp.146-170
           A detailed discussion of the relationship
       between Osborne's A Bond Honoured and Lope de
       Vega's La fianza satisfecha. "Where Osborne
       translates he does so with invigorating ruth-
       lessness and a firm grasp of essentials; where
       he alters the story, he tends to clarify causes
       but to obscure consequences. He preserves, even
       intensifies, the religious fervour of the origi-
       nal, but the meaning is radically altered and
       becomes extremely mysterious."

29 SHAYON, ROBERT LEWIS. "Luther, Whose Identity
       Crisis?" Saturday Review, LI (February 17,
       1968), 42
           Discusses the television adaptation of Luther.

30 SPACKS, PATRICIA MEYER. "Confrontation and Escape
       in Two Social Dramas." Modern Drama, XI (May
       1968), 61-72
           Compares Look Back in Anger with Ibsen's A
       Doll's House because both are concerned with
       types of social reformation. Osborne's play is
       inferior in characterization, diction, and
       ability to arouse audience response. Ibsen pre-
       sents awareness, while Osborne does not.

31 SPURLING, HILARY. "Ustiborne and Oskov." Specta-
       tor, CCXX (May 31, 1968), 752
           Time Present is "boring" and "damned fra-
       gile."

32 STYAN, J. L. The Dark Comedy: The Development of
      Modern Comic Tragedy. Cambridge: Cambridge Uni-
      versity Press, 1968, pp.117-118, 172, 257-258
          Brief comments on Look Back in Anger, The En-
      tertainer, and Luther as recent developments in
      modern comic tragedy.

33 TREWIN, J. C. "A Cocktail Party from Guinness."
      Illustrated London News, CCLII (June 8, 1968),
      41
          Time Present is monotonous, however "there
      is probably much in it for people more natural-
      ly sympathetic to Osborne's method."

34 _____. "Playboys and Indians." Illustrated Lon-
      don News, CCLIII (July 13, 1968), 30
          The Hotel in Amsterdam is "Osborne's most
      satisfying play." This is the first Osborne
      play that Trewin has liked.

35 TRUSSLER, SIMON. "British Neo-Naturalism." The
      Drama Review, XIII (Winter, 1968), 130-136
          Discussion of Osborne's effect on Wesker and
      the whole of modern drama. The foreshadowing
      of attitudes of contemporary prominence was the
      greatest contribution of Look Back in Anger.
      Osborne was able to show that the theatre could
      say something of importance about the condition
      of man.

36 TYNAN, KENNETH. "John Osborne Talks to Kenneth
      Tynan." London Observer (June 30, 1968), p.21
          In this first part of a two part interview
      Osborne's comments center primarily on the
      state of the contemporary theatre, his own work,
      his public image, his movies, Time Present, and
      his work in television.

37 _____. "John Osborne Talks to Kenneth Tynan."
    London Observer (July 7, 1968), p.21
        Continuation of Tynan's interview with Os-
    borne in which the main topics discussed are
    England, patriotism, student and youth rebel-
    lions, drugs, and the past.

38 _____. "John Osborne Talks to Kenneth Tynan--Can-
    didly." Atlas, XVI (September, 1968), 54-57
        A condensed reprint of Tynan's interview
    with Osborne that originally appeared in the
    London Observer.

39 WARDLE, IRVING. "Puzzling Split Between Old and
    New." London Times (May 24, 1968), p.7a
        Time Present is a curious combination of old
    and new styles and behavior. It is a confusing-
    ly closed play and not among Osborne's better
    works.

40 _____. "Osborne Offers an Angry Young Woman." New
    York Times (May 25, 1968), p.28:1
        Time Present is Osborne's "most selfconscious
    and stylistically fractured work to date."

41 _____. "Osborne's Curious Affinity." London Times
    (July 4, 1968), p.13f
        The Hotel in Amsterdam possesses a "curious
    affinity with Noel Coward's Design for Living
    in the portrayal of a developing friendship
    among people who make up their values from day
    to day."

42 _____. "The World of John Osborne." London Times
    (July 6, 1968), p.18e
        Osborne has always been a spokesman for his
    time and generally won praise from the London
    public for anything he presents. All of

WARDLE, IRVING (cont.)
Osborne's heroes have a peculiar relationship to the public temper, but in his new plays, Time Present and The Hotel in Amsterdam, a new hero arises, one that almost has to be identified with Osborne's personality. This hero is concerned with "what it costs to stay creatively alive in a society in which he finds nothing of creative value."

43 WEIGHTMAN, JOHN. "Grousers, Male and Female." Encounter, XXXI (September, 1968), 44-45
Extremely unfavorable review of Time Present and The Hotel in Amsterdam and a personal attack on Osborne.

44 WELLS, JOHN. "Music Music Music." Spectator, CCXXI (July 12, 1968), 61-62
Time Present is a "solid prop" of Osborne's greatness as a dramatist. The play is almost perfect, well constructed, possesses "masterly" dialogue, and is generally a great success.

A. Books--1969

1 BANHAM, MARTIN. Osborne. Edinburgh: Oliver and Boyd, 1969
The introduction of this book, which precedes individual discussions of Osborne's plays to 1968, is a defense of the playwright as more than an angry young man or a social reformer. Even though Osborne's drama is used as a weapon against those things in society that impede the individual's freedom, he alone has modernized the British theatre and brought it into the center of controversy.

ABOUT JOHN OSBORNE (1969)

2   CARTER, ALAN. <u>John Osborne</u>. Edinburgh: Oliver and
       Boyd, 1969
          Discusses all of Osborne's plays up to <u>The</u>
       <u>Hotel in Amsterdam</u> (1968) and includes a bio-
       graphical chapter and an extensive bibliography.
       Osborne is considered primarily as a playwright
       of social criticism. His most original contri-
       bution to the English theatre was bringing the
       word "love" back into vogue--the love between
       man and woman and the love between man and so-
       ciety. Osborne's main thrust is seen to be in
       an attempt to revise society, the element that
       focused attention upon him during the 1950's.

3   TRUSSLER, SIMON. <u>John Osborne</u>. London: Longmans,
       Green, 1969
          Critical and biographical discussion of Os-
       borne and his work from <u>Look Back in Anger</u> to
       <u>The Hotel in Amsterdam</u>. This thirty-two page
       pamphlet is part of the "Writer's and Their Work"
       series, number two-hundred thirteen.

4   _____. <u>The Plays of John Osborne: An Assessment</u>.
       London: Victor Gollancz, 1969
          An analysis of all of Osborne's plays to <u>The</u>
       <u>Hotel in Amsterdam</u>. Included are brief plot
       summaries, critical commentary, appraisal of
       Osborne's non-dramatic writings, and an exten-
       sive bibliography. Trussler attempts to avoid
       an overly biographical approach, which most
       critics have taken in relation to Osborne's
       drama. His main purpose is to establish Os-
       borne as a modern dramatist of the first rank
       and to provide a "companion" study of plays'
       thematic importance. Each play is taken indi-
       vidually with no consistent attempt to depict
       recurring themes or stylistic development.

B. Articles--1969

1 ALVAREZ, A. "John Osborne and the Boys at the
      Ball." New York Times (September 28, 1969), II,
      p.1:6
          An interview with Osborne prefaced by com-
      ments on his current economic affluence. Os-
      borne discusses A Patriot for Me, his attitude
      toward writing, and his current work.

2 BARNES, CLIVE. "Theater: A Patriot for Me Recalls
      the Decadence and Downfall of an Empire." New
      York Times (October 6, 1969), p.58:1. Re-
      printed in New York Theatre Critics' Reviews,
      XXX (October 13, 1969), 246
          Despite its faults, A Patriot for Me is an
      interesting and memorable play in which Os-
      borne's writing talents are clearly evident.

3 BRUSTEIN, ROBERT. The Third Theatre. New York:
      Alfred A. Knopf, 1969, pp.146-148
          Reprints Brustein's "Osborne's Elegaic
      Monody" from New Republic.

4 CAMERON, KENNETH M. AND THEODORE J. C. HOFFMAN. The
      Theatrical Response. London: Macmillan, 1969,
      pp.167, 191, 194
          Brief mention of Luther and Look Back in
      Anger.

5 CARNALL, GEOFFREY. "Saints and Human Beings: Orwell
      Osborne, and Ghandi" in Essays Presented to Amy
      G. Stock. Jaipur, India: Rajasthan University
      Press, 1969, pp.168-177. Reprinted in John Os-
      borne: LOOK BACK IN ANGER, A Casebook.
          A comparison of Orwell and Osborne with some
      remarks on Ghandi, especially in relation to

CARNALL, GEOFFREY (cont.)
Orwell's essay on Ghandi. All three are looking for some type of redemption in the world
through human strength.

6 CHAPMAN, JOHN. "Patriot for Me Goes Drag and Gets
Lost." New York Daily News (October 6, 1969).*
Reprinted in New York Theatre Critics' Reviews,
XXX (October 13, 1969), 245
The play is a total failure, but "from the
applause, there must have been some homos in the
big theater. More than some."

7 CLURMAN, HAROLD. "Theatre." Nation, CCIX (October
27, 1969), 451-452
Although A Patriot for Me is not Osborne's
best, the thesis of the "decadence and hypocrisy
of established empires" deserves praise. Clurman attempts to see the play as a total theatrical experience and finds that Osborne does not
attempt to focus on the entire decay of the sys-
tem, but on the career of one "not very extraor-
dinary officer."

8 COHN, RUBY. Currents in Contemporary Drama. Bloom-
ington: Indiana University Press, 1969, pp.5-6,
12-15, 123-124, 209
Brief biographical account and comment on
Brecht's influence on Osborne's Luther.

9 COOKE, RICHARD P. "Through Decadent Paces." Wall
Street Journal (October 7, 1969), p.22. Reprinted in New York Theatre Critics' Reviews,
XXX (October 13, 1969), 244-245
The play is well written and dramatically
sound except for its over-anxious attempts at
social criticism and a few technical errors.

10 CRINKLEY, RICHMOND. "The Loss of Privacy." <u>Na-</u>
       <u>tional Review</u>, XXI (December 30, 1969), 1334-
       1335
          Osborne's <u>A Patriot for Me</u> dwells on the
       "pathetic little moments of self-revelation"
       which have become almost commonplace in contem-
       porary society due to the electronic media.
       With all of this type of analysis going on
       around us, we might well wonder why we need it
       in the theatre.

11 ESSLIN, MARTIN. <u>Reflections: Essays on Modern Thea-</u>
       <u>tre</u>. Garden City: Doubleday, 1969, pp.78, 81,
       <u>84-85</u>, 167
          <u>Luther</u> and <u>A Patriot for Me</u> suffer from Os-
       borne's lack of understanding of the historical
       culture in which they are set. Brief mention
       of <u>Look Back in Anger</u> and <u>The World of Paul</u>
       <u>Slickey</u>.

12 _____. <u>The Theatre of the Absurd</u>. Garden City:
       Doubleday, 1969, pp.101-102, 379
          Brief comment on the controversy of Ionesco's
       statement that he saw social dramatists, such as
       Osborne, as lamentable conformists and mentions
       George Devine's defense that these dramatists
       write dramas about human values. The dream se-
       quence at the beginning of <u>Inadmissable Evi-</u>
       <u>dence</u> is used as an example of how absurd tech-
       niques infiltrate conventional drama.

13 GILL, BRENDAN. "In Old Vienna." <u>New Yorker</u>, XLV
       (October 11, 1969), 85
          <u>A Patriot for Me</u> is a waste of Osborne's
       talents even though the waste goes almost un-
       noticed because of Osborne's "O'Henry-like
       whiplash of a line."

14 GOLDMAN, WILLIAM. The Season: A Candid Look at
    Broadway. New York: Harcourt, Brace and World,
    1969, pp.41, 115, 318
        Brief information on Osborne in comments on
    other playwrights.

15 GOTTFRIED, MARTIN. "A Patriot for Me." Women's
    Wear Daily (October 6, 1969).* Reprinted in
    New York Theatre Critics' Reviews, XXX (October
    13, 1966)
        The play is a complete failure, much in line
    with the lack of dramatic ability found in Os-
    borne's previous work.

16 _____. Opening Nights: Theatrical Criticism of the
    Sixties. New York: G. P. Putnam, 1969
        Reprints Gottfried's review of Inadmissable
    Evidence from Women's Wear Daily.

17 HARRIS, LEONARD. "A Patriot for Me." New York
    Theatre Critics' Reviews, XXX (October 13, 1969),
    248
        Transcript of a television theatre review of
    October 5, 1969, which praises the play for hav-
    ing "meat," but it does not have enough "cre-
    scendo."

18 HASKELL, MOLLY. "Look Back in Drag." Village Voice
    (October 16, 1969), p.50
        Compared to Osborne's earlier plays, the
    characters in A Patriot for Me are "no longer
    created hot off it [Osborne's anger] but are
    second hand, infra-red versions of historical
    figures."

19 HEWES, HENRY. "Theater Paprika." Saturday Review,
    LII (October 18, 1969), 20
        The failure of A Patriot for Me in New York

HEWES, HENRY (cont.)
    was primarily due to its poor production, es-
    pecially staging it in a large musical comedy
    theatre rather than an intimate off-Broadway
    playhouse.

20 HUGHES, CATHERINE. "John Osborne's Generation Gap."
        America, CXXI (October 11, 1969), 295-297
        There has been a change in Osborne's dra-
    matic focus from being strictly anti-establish-
    ment in Look Back in Anger and gradually moving
    toward a more pro-establishment, anti-avant
    garde position in Time Present and The Hotel in
    Amsterdam.

21 KAUFFMAN, STANLEY. "On Theater." New Republic,
        CLXI (November 1, 1969), 22
        The idea in A Patriot for Me is "bleakly un-
    fulfilled," and it appears that Osborne was not
    able to make the transition from his earlier
    work with much success. He "simply seized the
    incident of the Redl scandal too quickly and
    wrote, no matter how long it took him, too
    early."

22 KENNEDY, ANDREW K. "Old and New in London Now."
        Modern Drama, XI (February, 1969), 437-446
        A review essay of current London productions
    including Osborne's Time Present and The Hotel
    in Amsterdam. "For Osborne, who has some of
    Chekov's compassion but none of his inwardness
    or artistic detachment, cannot face the direct
    portrayal of boredom and emptiness. . . . The
    two latest plays show how difficult it is for
    Osborne to develop a consistent theatrical style
    for the contemporary scene, expressing both the
    reality and the factitiousness of the present
    time."

ABOUT JOHN OSBORNE (1969)

23 KERR, WALTER. "Why Has Osborne Taken the Trouble?"
     New York Times (October 12, 1969), II, p.1:1.
     Reprinted in New York Theatre Critics' Reviews,
     XXX (October 13, 1969), 247-248
        A Patriot for Me seems to have no real point
     and no real purpose, which is unusual for Os-
     borne.

24 KROLL, JACK. "Decline and Fall." Newsweek, LXXIV
     (October 18, 1969), 129
        A Patriot for Me is a complete success. The
     twenty scenes of the play follow Redl's decline
     against a background of general moral decay
     that ends with Redl's suicide and the end of
     the Austro-Hungarian Empire in 1914.

25 "Osborne for TV." London Times (May 9, 1969), p.8g
        Notice that Osborne has signed to do a ninety
     minute drama for the National Broadcasting Com-
     pany.

26 "Wrath at the Helm?" London Times (May 26, 1969),
     p.7c
        Compared to the younger British generation,
     who possess a "cinderella spirit," Osborne's
     Look Back in Anger seems misguided.

27 "Moscow Looks Back in Anger." London Times (Decem-
     ber 19, 1969), p.7e
        In a Pravda article by Aleksandr Chakovsky,
     Osborne and Braine are both accused of giving
     themselves up to the established western ide-
     ology and retreating from the tenets of the
     angry young man movement. This Russian attack
     was "probably connected with the recent pro-
     tests in the west about the expulsion of Alex-
     andr Solzhenitsyn."

28 NEWMAN, EDWIN. "A Patriot for Me." New York Thea-
      tre Critics' Reviews, XXX (October 13, 1969),
      248
        Transcript of a television theatre review
      which finds some faults in the play, but has
      general praise. This review was broadcast on
      October 5, 1969.

29 NOBILE, PHILLIP. "The Stage." Commonweal, XCI
      (November 7, 1969), 185-186
        "John Osborne's Patriot, a dreadful spy-homo-
      sexual melodrama, bores from within." Nothing
      in the play works very well, especially Os-
      borne's cliche-ridden portrayal of homosexuality.

30 O'BRIEN, CHARLES H. "Osborne's Luther and the Hu-
      manistic Tradition." Renascence, XXI (Winter,
      1969), 59-63
        On several points, Osborne's portrayal of
      Luther's character and his religious action
      agrees with earlier humanist critics such as
      Erasmus. Although in the play Luther tends to
      be more modern than his true medievalism would
      have allowed, because Osborne's conception of
      his character "is good theater and rings true
      to many modern cultivated persons, it will like-
      ly assume a prominent place in the gallery of
      Reformation portraits."

31 O'CONNOR, JOHN J. "The Three Faces of John Osborne."
      Audience, VI (Spring, 1969), 108-113
        In his first three plays, Osborne presents
      three masks of personality (George Dillon, Jimmy
      Porter, and Archie Rice) each being contradic-
      tions of the other. All are united, though,
      through Osborne's talent and knowledge of the
      theatre and audience manipulation.

32 ROLLINS, RONALD G. "Carroll and Osborne: Alice and
      Alison in Wild Wonderlands." Forum, VII (1969),
      16-20
         Rollins finds distinct parallels between Look
      Back in Anger and Alice in Wonderland.
      "Carroll's fantasy serves as a kind of framing
      device for the dramatic situation. . . . Os-
      borne consciously derives character, conduct,
      landscape, themes, and imagery from Carroll's
      classic."

33 "Viennese Drag." Time, XCIV (October 17, 1969),
      71
         A Patriot for Me was written with a "high-
      school-pageant ideal of history." This makes
      the play confusing and, unless the audience
      assumes that there is importance in the theme
      that homosexuals make poor security risks,
      pointless. The only good Osborne play is the
      one in which the playwright himself is the cen-
      tral character.

34 TUCKER, JOHN BARTHOLOMEW. "A Patriot for Me." New
      York Theatre Critics' Reviews, XXX (October 13,
      1969), 248
         Transcript of a television theatre review
      (October 5, 1969). "A Patriot for Me is a dead-
      ly, deathly dull play."

35 WATTS, RICHARD. "The Case of an Austrian Traitor."
      New York Post (October 6, 1969).* Reprinted in
      New York Theatre Critics' Reviews, XXX (October
      13, 1969), 244
         A Patriot for Me is not a very good play,
      but whatever value it does have is almost exclu-
      sively due to the production and direction.

36 WEST, ANTHONY. "A Patriot for Me: Sedated Teddy-
        bear." Vogue, CLIV (November 15, 1969), 58
            Questions the value of a play based on the
        life of a "third-rate human." The character of
        Redl never achieves importance, the action re-
        mains uniformly slow, and neither is helped by
        Maximillian Schell's performance which "sug-
        gests a heavily sedated Teddybear."

37 WILLIAMS, RAYMOND. Drama From Ibsen to Brecht.
        New York: Oxford University Press, 1969, pp.318-
        322
            Look Back in Anger is the first breakthrough
        in the English theatre of the cultural idiom of
        the isolation of a "trapped identifiable group."
        The play does not direct the reader to a specif-
        ic interpretation of its case, but is markedly
        formless in its conclusions.

38 ZEIGER, HENRY A. "Three From Act, Plus One." New
        Leader, LII (October 27, 1969), 25
            A Patriot for Me is "a trifle thin," lacking
        the dramatic intensity of Osborne's earlier
        work.

A. Books--1970

None

B. Articles--1970

1 DRIVER, TOM F. Romantic Quest and Modern Query.
        New York: Delacorte, 1970, pp.455-456
            Brief mention of Osborne in the "Epilogue."
        Driver finds the early work of Osborne and
        Wesker to be more of "sociological importance
        than theatrical." Both authors have turned away
        from their initial interests and experimented

DRIVER, TOM F. (cont.)
   with various forms, but Osborne was "all the
   while cultivating his principal strength, which
   is the composition of speeches of unusually
   powerful rhetoric."

2 DUNKLEY, CHRIS. "The Right Prospectus." London
   Times (October 23, 1970), p.15g
      This television play has no central focus and
   seems to skip from one subject of disgust to another.

3 FABER, M. O. "The Character of Jimmy Porter: An
   Approach to Look Back in Anger." Modern Drama,
   XIII (May, 1970), 67-77
      Psychoanalytic critique of Jimmy Porter. He
   is seen as "an orally fixated neurotic," whose
   false anger arise from a projection of his
   shortcomings on to the external world. The play
   is a portrayal of a neurotic individual, rather
   than a criticism of society.

4 KARRAFALT, DAVID H. "The Social Theme in Osborne's
   Plays." Modern Drama, XIII (May, 1970), 78-82
      Discusses the theme of man's isolation and
   despair throughout Osborne's work, particularly
   in relation to Luther and Look Back in Anger.
   His plays are written for those who do feel emo-
   tions and compassion and against those who do
   not. Also, they are a reflection of the reality
   of modern man's separation.

5 LAHR, JOHN. Up Against the Fourth Wall. New York:
   Grove Press, 1970
      Reprints Lahr's essay "Poor Johnny One-Note"
   from the Evergreen Review.

6 LEECH, CLIFFORD. The Dramatist's Experience. New
       York: Barnes and Noble, 1970, p.140
          Brief comparison of Archie Rice to Gormless
       Gordon in David Storey's Radcliffe.

7 LITTLE, STUART W. AND ARTHUR CANTOR. The Playmakers.
       New York: Norton, 1970, pp.72, 171, 291, 301
          Brief comments on the Broadway reception of
       Look Back in Anger, Luther, A Patriot for Me,
       and Inadmissable Evidence.

8 "Royal College of Art." London Times (March 19,
       1970), p.12b
          Osborne is to be made an honorary Doctor of
       the Royal College of Art.

9 "Hand-picked." London Times (June 27, 1970), p.8g
          Discusses Osborne's movie plans.

10 "Osborne's Second Film Role." London Times (August
       10, 1970), p.5d
          Osborne is cast for a role in "Carter."

11 "Osborne the Romantic." London Times (August 28,
       1970), p.6f
          General article on Osborne's career based on
       a recent interview. Discusses his movie role
       in "Carter," public image, and personality.

12 ROBSON, W. W. Modern English Literature. London:
       Oxford University Press, 1970, pp.116, 157-158
          The initial appeal of Osborne, especially in
       Look Back in Anger and The Entertainer, was
       political, but with the perspective of his later
       work Osborne is seen as less political and more
       concerned with "domestic obsessions."

13 SIGAL, CLANCY. "Looking Back Without Anger." Com-
      monweal, XCII (May 8, 1970), 186-188
          Traces some of the cultural circumstances
      surrounding the beginning of the angry young
      man cult and relates what those who were in-
      volved have been doing since.

14 SIMON, JOHN. "Theatre Chronicle." Hudson Review,
      XXIII, (Spring, 1970), 91
          The David Merrick revival of A Patriot for Me
      reminded "us how quickly mores--in society, on
      stage--can change. . . . It also shows Osborne
      transformed from a strident proletarian rebel
      into a smug, conservative arrioiste."

A. Books--1971

None

B. Articles--1971

1 DAWSON, HELEN. "Osborne's Island." London Observer
     (August 22, 1971), p.24
         West of Suez contains some of Osborne's best
     writing and is a considerable step forward from
     The Hotel in Amsterdam. Osborne "takes us by
     the throat and memorably captures the submerged
     panic that accompanies a time of change."

2 GILMAN, RICHARD. Common and Uncommon Masks. New
     York: Random House, 1971, pp.114-115
         Reprints Gilman's "A Man For These Times"
     from Newsweek.

3 HOBSON, HAROLD. "Osborne's Suez: Light on the Rul-
     ing Class." Christian Science Monitor (August
     21, 1971), p.4
         The replacement of the old order with the new

HOBSON, HAROLD (cont.)
   carries antithetical elements. Osborne's portrayal of this dialectical confrontation and his
   demonstrated dramatic prowess make this play
   "one of his finest works."

4 HURREN, KENNETH. "Look Forward in Anguish." Spec-
      tator, CCXXVII (August 28, 1971), 313-314
         The play is ambiguous and confusing in its
      thematic direction. Osborne seems to be re-
      treating from his commitment to social reform
      and in the retreat is presenting his own split
      opinion in West of Suez.

5 KRETZMER, HERBERT. "Old Angry Still Leads the
      Pack." London Daily Express (August 18, 1971),
      p.13
         West of Suez drags at times and uses the
      typical objects of Osborne's invective, but it
      clearly demonstrates with its dramatic power and
      "dialogue that echoes the mood and malady of our
      rotting age" that Osborne is still the leading
      British dramatist.

6 LEWIS, ALLAN. The Contemporary Theater. New York:
      Crown, 1971, pp.315-335
         General discussion of Osborne's plays from
      Look Back in Anger to The Hotel in Amsterdam.
      Look Back in Anger's significance was widespread
      and heralded a new age for British drama, but
      Osborne soon rejected the "angry" stance.
      Luther was Osborne's "fumbling" attempt in the
      Brechtian mode and a dramatic failure.

7 "Suez Style." London Times (July 13, 1971), p.12g
         Discussion of the pre-performance aspects of
      West of Suez.

8 NIGHTINGALE, BENEDICT. "Osborne's Old Times." <u>New
     Statesman</u>, LXXXII (August 27, 1971), 277
         An expression of the growing disappointment
     in Osborne as a cult protest leader, a protest
     for reform that was born from <u>Look Back in
     Anger</u>. Osborne's position has grown more con-
     servative and less involved with his original
     problems and concerns. <u>West of Suez</u> is the
     final proof of his new position. "Isn't it as
     if Jimmy Porter made good, turned his coat,
     accepted his knighthood and became joint master
     of the Quorn?"

9 SHEED, WILFRED. <u>The Morning After</u>. New York:
     Farrar, Straus and Giroux, 1971, pp.154-156
         Reprints Sheed's "Johnny One-Note" from <u>Com-
     monweal</u>.

10 "Pick of the London Season." <u>Time</u>, XCVIII (August
     30, 1971), 48
         The play is evidence of Osborne's shift to a
     conservative political position, especially
     when compared to <u>Look Back in Anger</u>. Like all
     of his plays, <u>West of Suez</u> has no dramatic co-
     herency but a total concentration on a single
     character.

11 TREWIN, J. C. "Month of the Ravens." <u>Illustrated
     London News</u>, CCLIX (October, 1971), 56
         Brief and mixed review. <u>West of Suez</u> is
     "hard to classify" and somewhat confusing.

12 WARDLE, IRVING. "<u>Inadmissable Evidence</u>." <u>London
     Times</u> (February 3, 1971), p.11a
         In this revival of the play, it is clear that
     <u>Inadmissable Evidence</u> represents the drama of
     the sixties just as <u>Look Back in Anger</u> repre-

WARDLE, IRVING (cont.)
    sented the drama of the fifties. As of now,
    Osborne is the only British playwright "capable
    of creating modern British heroes."

13   _____. "West of Suez." London Times (August 18,
        1971), p.8c
            The obvious influence on the play is Os-
        borne's interest in Chekov and the Chekovian
        dramatic style. However, the play is "deeply
        disappointing" because of Osborne's inability
        to move away from the "temporarily privileged
        egotist" nature of his characters.

14   _____. "West of Suez." London Times (October 7,
        1971), p.11g
            Compared with the other current plays on the
        West End, Osborne's looks good. But it still
        possesses all of the flaws of the egocentric
        character, over-written dialogue, and thematic
        vagueness that it had in its original production
        at the Royal Court.

15 WEIGHTMAN, JOHN. "Post-Imperial Blues." Encounter,
        XXXVII (November, 1971), 56-58
            When the first scene finished it appeared
        that Osborne may have taken a completely new
        direction, one almost Chekovian. But it soon
        was "clear that West of Suez is basically the
        usual Osborne piece, with a big self-loving,
        self-hating character rampaging at the center."

16 WILMETH, DON. "Theatre in Review." Educational
        Theatre Journal, XII (1971), 466
            In the major character, Wyatt, Osborne's
        greatness as a writer can be seen, but West of
        Suez is "static" and "a rather meaningless ex-
        position."

John Osborne: A Reference Guide

AO   ABOUT JOHN OSBORNE (1972)

A. Books--1972

None

B. Articles--1972

1 BIRNBAUM, JESSE. "The Audience as Victim." Time,
     C (December 25, 1972), 36
       "A Sense of Detachment is in many ways a mis-
chievous experiment in audience participation."
The "message" of the play is frequently lost in
the audience's extreme reactions.

2 BROWN, JOHN RUSSELL. Theatre Language: A Study of
     Arden, Osborne, Pinter and Wesker. London:
     Allen Lane The Penguin Press, 1972, pp.118-157
       Brown attempts to show through a rather de-
tailed analysis of Osborne's drama why and how
these plays "work" on the stage and have such a
tremendous popular appeal. Primarily, he concludes that Osborne involves the audience in
the despair--or picture of despair--of his characters, through the believability of their
"word" and their "silence." "At the center of
Osborne's revelation of character-in-defeat is
a realization of the need for courage to con-
tinue with the most basic elements of life that
are, by the last scenes, known only too well."

3 BRUSTEIN, ROBERT. "Subjects of Scandal and Con-
     cern." London Observer (December 17, 1972),
     p.32
       The interest of A Sense of Detachment is in
exploring the overly familiar distinctions between the theatre and reality. Osborne's play
is poor. "It shows us Mr. Osborne's Muse in a
suspended state . . . tapping her foot while
waiting for inspiration to flow."

134

4 HURREN, KENNETH. "Osborne and Arden." Spectator,
      CCXXIX (December 9, 1972), 934
         In A Sense of Detachment, Osborne apparently
      wishes to criticize the present state of English
      theatre and, especially, Beckett and Pinter.
      "Osborne has not quite mastered the trick of
      writing about bores and boredom without being
      ineffably boring himself."

5 KRETZMER, HERBERT. "Making Hedda a Little Less
      Hateful." London Daily Express (June 29, 1972),
      p.10
         "Osborne seems to have directed the play
      towards our own age," a pleasant handling of a
      "boring masterpiece like Hedda Gabler."

6 MORTIMER, JOHN. "Bed and Bored." London Observer
      (July 2, 1972), p.29
         Osborne's adaptation strips Hedda Gabler of
      its "literary trimmings" and allows us to feel
      the play with a fresh emotional impact.

7 ROY, EMIL. British Drama Since Shaw. Carbondale:
      University of Southern Illinois, 1972, pp.100,
      106, 115, 123-124, 128
         A discussion of Osborne from Look Back in
      Anger to The Hotel in Amsterdam. Roy feels that
      Inadmissable Evidence is Osborne's "firmest
      achievement to date" and in the depiction of
      the angst of modern isolation he is rivaled only
      by Harold Pinter.

8 WARDLE, IRVING. "Hedda Gabler." London Times (June
      30, 1972), p.11
         "It is a loving piece of work in which one
      senses Osborne trying to master an obsession
      with the play and explain its mysteries to his
      own satisfaction. It can be taken as a faithful
      version of Hedda Gabler."

B9   ABOUT JOHN OSBORNE (1972)

9   ____. "Unnamed Figures in a Limbo Scene." London
     Times (December 5, 1972), p.14
          A Sense of Detachment is mired with redundant
     cliches and directionless anger. "You might
     look at the piece as a terminal point of Os-
     borne's derision which has now spread from the
     world outside to the theatrical process itself."

10   ____. "Epitaph for George Dillon." London Times
     (December 8, 1972), p.13
          In the original production of the play, the
     openness of artistic and humanistic possibili-
     ties at the end of the play was silenced by the
     nature of Dillon's presentation. "In view of
     Osborne's age when he wrote it and of his sub-
     sequent development, the piece is astonishingly
     fairminded.

Selected Non-English Criticism

1 ADANIA, ALF. "Osborne azi, la Amsterdam." Romania
     Literară, V (January, 1969), 22

2 ADELL, A. "Lope, Osborne y los criticos." Insula,
     XXII (June, 1967), 7

3 ANIKST, A. "Ot Osborna k Mersu." Teatăr, VI
     (1969), 147-157

4 BONNERAT, LOUIS. "John Osborne." Etudes Anglaises,
     X (1957), 378-391

5 HAHNLOSER-INGOLD, MARGRIT. Das Englische Theater
     und Bert Brecht. Bern: Francke, 1970

6 IHLENHELD, KURT. "Osborne's Luther." Eckart
     (1961-1962), 312-315

ABOUT JOHN OSBORNE

7 KATO, KYOHEI. "An Essay on John Osborne" in Col-
   lected Essays by Members of the Faculty. No.
   13. Kyoritsu, Japan: Kyoritsu Junior College,
   1969, 103-109

8 ODAJIMA, YUJI. J. Osborne. Tokyo: Kenkyusha, 1970

9 OPPEL, HORST. Das Moderne Englische Drama. Berlin:
   Erich Schmidt, 1963

10 OSZTOVITS, LEVENTE. "John Osborne" in Az angel
    irodalom a husz adik században. Eds. Laszlo
    Báti and István Kristó-Nagy. Budapest: Gondo-
    lat, 1970, 231-58

11 PEINERT, DETRICH. "'Bea' und 'Squirrel' in John Os-
    borne's Look Back in Anger." Literatur in Wis-
    senschaft und Unterricht, I (1968), 117-122

12 SAHL, HANS. "John Osborne." Welt und Wort, XIV
    (1959), 36-37

13 SCHMIDT, K. D. Kirchengeschicte. Gottingen: 1960.

14 SELZ, JEAN. "John Osborne et Jimmy Porter." Les
    Lettres Nouvelles, LXI (June, 1958), 908-911

15 SERVADIO, GAIA. "Il dandy con il mitra spara e
    salve." La Fiera Litteraire (August 1, 1968),
    pp.14-16

16 SHOSTAKOV, D. "Monologi Dzhona Osborna." Inostran-
    naya literatura, VII (1967), 112-116

17 STEFANOV, VASIL. "Spoluki na mladostta. Piesata
    'Osbárne se s gnjai nazad' vav Varnenskija
    dramat teatár." Teatár, XXI, 3 (1968), 43-44

ABOUT JOHN OSBORNE

18 TYNAN, KENNETH. "Perche oggi tutti discons 'noi' e
    maj 'io' conversazione con John Osborne." La
    Fiera Litteraire (September 26, 1968), pp.2-4

19 VALLETTE, JACQUES. "Lettres Anglo-Saxonnes: La
    Societe Anglaise et le Theatre de John Osborne."
    Mercure de France, CCCXXXIII (June, 1958), 342-
    346

20 VAN DE PERRE, H. John Osborne, boze jonge man.
    The Hague: Tielt, 1962

21 WEST, ALTICK. "John Osborne." Filologiai Kozlony,
    IX (January-June, 1963), 129-134

Index

This index is intended to provide access to the information contained in section two of the bibliography, "About John Osborne." Entries are arranged alphabetically by author and work in one sequence. The Index gives the location of items by particular authors who have written about Osborne and also, all of the entries under the titles of Osborne's works that specifically deal with individual works are listed. The listing of each entry is followed by a notation of where the work can be found. Thus, the first entry appears as:

Adelman, Irving 1967 B1

Thus under the year 1967, in section two, Irving Adelman's work on John Osborne will be the first entry listed under "Articles." All book entries (those books which are exclusively concerned with Osborne) are given "A" numbers; all article entries (which include not only articles, but reviews and parts of books dealing with Osborne) are given "B" numbers.

INDEX OF AUTHORS AND WORKS

INDEX OF AUTHORS AND WORKS

INDEX OF AUTHORS AND WORKS

INDEX OF AUTHORS AND WORKS

JOHN OSBORNE: A REFERENCE GUIDE

INDEX OF AUTHORS AND WORKS

Dukore, Bernard	1966 B15
Duncan, Ronald	1960 B1
Dunkley, Chris	1970 B2
Dupee, F. W.	1958 B23; 1965 B9
Duprey, Richard A.	1963 B8
Dworkin, Rita	1967 B1
Dyson, A. E.	1959 B9
Elsom, John	1966 B16
Entertainer, The	1957 B5, B11, B21, B23, B31, B33, B50, B52, B60, B63, B64, B65, B66, B67, B69, B74, B75; 1958 B1, B2, B4, B5, B10, B11, B13, B16, B18, B19, B21, B22, B24, B30, B35, B37, B39, B46, B47, B48, B50, B51, B55, B59, B63, B64, B65, B66, B67, B68, B71, B72, B74; 1959 B4, B19; 1961 B2, B7, B19; 1962 B3, B9, B17, B18; 1964 B3, B4, B9, B24, B27; 1965 B1, B5, B6, B8, B29, B44; 1966 B20, B44; 1967 B1, B2, B6; 1968 A1, B26, B32; 1969 A1, A2, A3, A4, B31; 1970 B6, B11; 1971 B6; 1972 B2, B7
Epitaph for George Dillon	1957 B4, B10, B29; 1958 B3, B5, B6, B11, B12, B14, B19, B22, B26, B27, B28, B31, B34, B36, B42, B45, B46, B49, B53, B54, B57, B58, B60, B66, B69,

INDEX OF AUTHORS AND WORKS

INDEX OF AUTHORS AND WORKS

INDEX OF AUTHORS AND WORKS

INDEX OF AUTHORS AND WORKS

INDEX OF AUTHORS AND WORKS

INDEX OF AUTHORS AND WORKS

INDEX OF AUTHORS AND WORKS

INDEX OF AUTHORS AND WORKS

INDEX OF AUTHORS AND WORKS

INDEX OF AUTHORS AND WORKS

Thompson, John	1959 B28
Time Present	1968 B1, B4, B7, B8, B9, B10, B15, B17, B19, B22, B27, B31, B33, B36, B39, B40, B42, B43, B44; 1969 A1, A2, A3, A4, B20, B22; 1971 B6; 1972 B2
Tom Jones	1961 B34, B36; 1962 B11, B12; 1963 B1, B7, B11, B15, B16, B22, B25, B30, B33, B36, B37, B46, B47; 1964 B6, B19; 1966 B4; 1968 B3
Trewin, J. C.	1957 B63, B64, B65; 1959 B30; 1961 B24; 1962 B19; 1964 B25; 1965 B44; 1966 B46; 1968 B33, B34; 1971 B11
Tricker, John Bartholomew	1969 B34
Trilling, Ossia	1960 B12; 1966 B45
Trussler, Simon	1966 B47; 1968 B35; 1969 A3, A4
Turnstile, M.	1966 B48
Tyler, Gary R.	1966 B12
Tynan, Kenneth	1956 B15; 1957 B66; 1958 B70, B71; 1961 B25; 1962 B20; 1964 B24; 1965 B45; 1967 B20; 1968 B36, B37, B38
Wain, John	1957 B67

INDEX OF AUTHORS AND WORKS